RAIL CENTRES:
READING
LAURENCE WATERS

RAIL CENTRES:
READING
LAURENCE WATERS

LONDON

IAN ALLAN LTD

Front endpaper:
The newly completed Western Tower dominates the skyline as Brush prototype Type 4 No D0280 *Falcon* stands at the up platform with the 8.00am Hereford-Paddington on 8 May 1967.
D. Cross

Rear endpaper:
This lovely view shows 'Britannia' No 70019 *Lightning* passing Reading West Junction with the 5.50pm service from Paddington to Swansea on 10 September 1959. *C. J. Blay*

Previous page, right:
'Star' class No 4004 *Morning Star* awaits departure from Reading with a down Worcester service on 5 August 1939. *V. R. Webster*

Previous page, left:
One of the last up broad gauge expresses, hauled by Gooch 4-4-2 *Bulkeley*, is seen passing through Sonning on Friday 20 May 1892.
Real Photos

to
David Kozlow

Photographs from the Locomotive & General Railway Photographs collection appear courtesy of David & Charles Ltd.

First published 1990

ISBN 0 7110 1937 1

Published by Ian Allan Ltd, Shepperton, Surrey; and printed by Ian Allan Printing Ltd at their works at Coombelands in Runnymede, England

Contents

Sources and Acknowledgements

I would like to thank the following individuals for their help with both information and photographs: B. Morrison, R. C. Riley, C. Haydon, B. Davis, R. Ruffell, J. Hewett, C. R. L. Coles, B. D. Stoyel, D. Tuck, D. Parker, P. Kelley, V. R. Webster, A. Summerfield, D. Castle, M. Yarwood, G. A. Carpenter, D. Collins, J. Bondreau, M. Mensing, Janet Heyhoe and Maurice Leach.

Also the Great Western Trust, the Ian Allan Library, the Industrial Railway Society, the Signalling Record Society, Photomatic, Lens of Sutton, Berkshire County Libraries, Nabisco UK Ltd, CEGB and British Gas.

Special thanks are due to Danny Martin and his staff at British Rail, Reading, to Rosemary Painter and Andrew Hall for checking the manuscript, Lesley Annetts for the diagrams and to Tony Harden, Jack Hewett and Ray Ruffell for their help throughout the project.

Introduction

Reading, the county town of Berkshire, was known for many years as the town of the three Bs: Bulbs, Biscuits and Beer. Today only the last of these is still produced in the town, but these industries and the town itself owed much of their expansion to the arrival of the Great Western and South Eastern Railway companies in 1840 and 1849 respectively. The establishment of the Great Western signal works at Caversham Road increased the town's importance on the railway map, and with the completion of the Berks & Hants route, Reading became a major junction and one of the most important centres on the system. The rundown of the railways during the 1960s and 1970s saw much of Reading's goods traffic disappear, with many of the local yards. The 'Southern' side suffered badly, with the closure of both the station and locomotive depot. The last decade has seen the old signal works completely obliterated.

Today the commercial nature of the town has changed, with the emphasis now firmly established in finance and insurance. The High Speed revolution of the 1970s has placed Reading within 25min of London, and the recent refurbishment of the station has once again put Reading to the forefront of Western Region operations as not only the busiest station, but arguably the most important centre on the Region.

Below:
Railways around Reading.

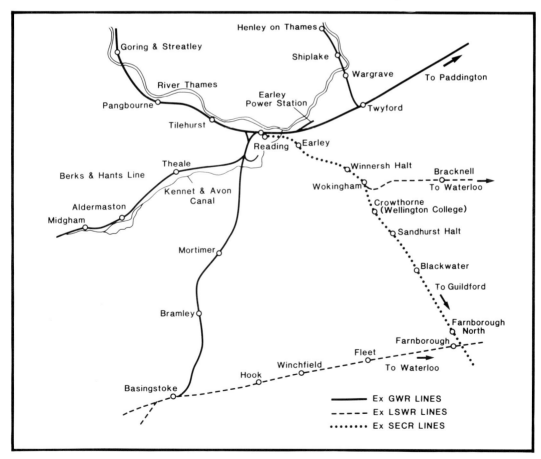

The Growth of the Railway at Reading

Reading, the county town of Berkshire and once royal borough of the Saxon Kingdom of Wessex stands a little over 100ft above sea level on a small ridge where 'the clear Kennet overtakes, His lord, the stately Thames'. The town has long been synonymous with both biscuits and beer, the former sadly now no longer produced in the town. These products, however, were relatively new to Reading, for in its earlier days it was an important centre for commercial trading, notably of cloth, in fact it was said for many years that the town 'standith by clothing'.

There is much evidence of early settlements here, some of which are pre stone age; however, the name Reading appears to have derived from Saxon times. The *Saxon Chronicle* relates that in AD 871, Readingum was raided by a Danish army. The name itself has possibly derived from the old English word Reada, whose people or followers are known as Readingas. The *Doomsday Book* lists both a Manor and a borough at Reddinges.

Apart from its early centre for the cloth trade, the town gained extra importance with the foundation by Henry I in 1121 of a Cluniac Abbey. After his death in France, the king's corpse was returned to England and was subsequently buried in the abbey. It was also here that a monk is reputed to have written the oldest known part-song in the English language, 'Sumer is a comen in'. The abbey was dismantled during the 16th century, and in 1786 a human hand, thought by some to be the hand of St James, was found by some workmen, hidden in the church wall. Today only a few remains of the abbey can still be seen, the most notable being the fine 13th century gatehouse in Forbury Street, which was restored by George Gilbert Scott in 1861.

By the 19th century the cloth trade had declined, and with the opening of the Kennet & Avon canal in 1810, the town became an important centre for the corn trade. Several schemes had been suggested, from as early as Elizabethan times to link the Avon with the Thames. This dream was finally realised

Left:
The entrance to the Great Western station at Reading.
Author's collection

Above:
A view of Broad Street, Reading, around the turn of the century. On the left is a Great Western delivery cart belonging to C. G. Ayres, the local goods agent, whilst in the centre the statue of George Palmer surveys the scene. It was erected by the town council in 1891, but was removed in 1930 to allow for road improvements, and today stands in Palmer Park. *B. Davis collection*

with the Royal Assent of the Avon Navigation Bill of 1712. This promoted the clearing of the River Avon to allow navigation to take place between the City Weir, Bath and Hanham Mills (Bristol). Work started during April 1724 and was finished and the link open to navigation by 15 December 1727. The second stage of the link was forged with the Royal Assent on 21 September 1715 of the Kennet Navigation Bill, to improve the Kennet between High Bridge Reading and Newbury, thus allowing navigation between these two points. After numerous problems it was opened to traffic on 1 June 1723, although not finally completed until the May of the following year. The new cuts and canals reduced the old river distance between Reading and Newbury to 18½ miles, only one mile or so more than the turnpike road. Some idea of the problems of this section can be gleaned from the fact that the canal rose in level from Reading by some 134ft, this being achieved by the construction of some 20 locks. The final link, the Western Canal, was proposed in 1770, by the then proprietor of the Kennet Canal Co, Frances Page, and by the time the Bill to build this section was promoted the name had been changed to the Kennet & Avon Canal Co. Work was started under the control of engineer John Rennie during October 1774, being finally completed and opened for through navigation over the 86½ miles between Reading and Hanham on 31 December 1810. The 57-mile link between Newbury and Bath certainly passed through some undulating countryside, which necessitated the construction of some 79 locks. The most spectacular section was at Devizes where the canal drops 140ft down Caen Hill via 17 successive locks. Over the next 30 years the canal brought increasing prosperity to Reading, together with a steady rise in the population as the following figures show:

1801: 9,400
1811: 10,800
1821: 12,900

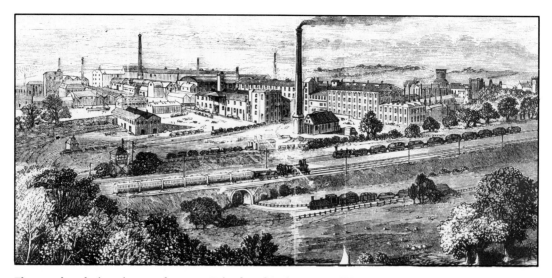

The canal and river journey between Bristol and London was not without its problems. Records show that the journey times were painfully slow and that in winter frosts regularly closed the canal, whilst in the summer both the canal and the Thames in particular suffered from low water levels holding up boats for weeks. It was against these problems that the Great Western Railway was formed. Probably the first information that the ordinary townsfolk of Reading gleaned about the new railway came from the advertisements placed in the *Reading Mercury* and the *Berkshire Chronicle* during August 1833, inviting subscribers to the new company. The prospectus stated that the cost of the 120-mile line would be £2,805,330, and that some £3,000,000 would have to be raised in shares of £100 each. The failure of this first Bill did not deter the company, and a second and this time successful Bill received Royal Assent in August 1835. This success was not without some strong support from the town of Reading itself in the form of a petition from the Mayor and burgesses in favour of the new railway. This support had been gained from a meeting held on 6 March 1834 at the Reading Town Hall. The meeting attended by the Mayor and 140 burgesses was addressed by the company secretary Charles Saunders, he stated that 'the town would be brought within one and a half-two hours of London instead of five at present and that the coming of the railway would increase the prosperity of the Town'. The local dignitaries it seems were far sighted enough to heed his words, for it was the arrival of the railway that produced the greatest influence on the growth of the town in both population and trade over the ensuing years. By 1842, only two years after its opening, the population had risen to some 22,000, and by the turn of the century stood at 75,214. It is worth mentioning that, although the town supported the new railway, some of the smaller landowners in

the county did not. A report in the *Reading Mercury* states that over 30 of them met at the Bear Inn at Reading on 9 December 1833 to voice their opposition to the scheme. This opposition was short lived, for by the time the work was ready to start in the Reading area, most if not all of them had sold out.

The Great Western reached Reading on 30 March 1840 with the opening of the line between here and Twyford. Brunel's great route from London to Bristol was eventually completed in nine stages. The first of these from Bishops Road (Paddington) to Taplow (Maidenhead) opened on 4 June 1838. This small station remained the terminus of the line for over a year until the second section, between Taplow and Twyford, was opened for passenger traffic on 1 July 1839. Such was the interest being shown at Reading, that a new stagecoach service known as 'The Railway' was soon inaugurated to run firstly between Reading and Maidenhead station and then when the line was extended westwards, from Reading to Twyford to connect with the trains. The section between Twyford and Reading was the third stage to open and from 30 March until 1 June 1840, when services were extended through to Steventon, trains terminated here. Progress continued and just over one year later, on 30 June 1841, the line was duly opened through to Bristol.

This remarkable route is, of course, famous for its easy gradients, with the station at Reading itself being built on the level. To achieve this locally was no mean feat as to the east the route had to bisect the hill at Sonning. Brunel's orginal intention, in order to maintain the easy gradient of 1 in 1,320 from Twyford, was to take the route to the north of Sonning and carry the line through the hill by way of a tunnel at nearby Holme Park, which would have been approximately 5/8 of a mile in length. After much thought Brunel made the decision to alter the

GREAT WESTERN RAILWAY.

LONDON TO BRISTOL.

DOWN FROM PADDINGTON TO	Departure from Paddington	UP TO PADDINGTON FROM	Departure from Wootton Basset road.
	h. m.		h. m.
Wootton Basset road, A.M.	8. 0	Wootton Basset road, A.M.	2.30
Maidenhead	8.30	*(Mail Train.)*	
Wootton Basset road	9. 0	Reading	—
Wootton Basset road	10. 0	Slough	—
Slough	10 30	Maidenhead	—
Wootton Basset road	12. 0	Wootton Basset road	8.30
Slough	1 30	Reading	—
Wootton Basset road	2. 0	Wootton Basset road	10.15
Wootton Basset road	4. 0	Wootton Basset road	11.30
Slough, P.M.	4 30	Slough	—
Reading	5. 0	Wootton Basset road, P.M.	1.15
Maidenhead	6. 0	Wootton Basset road	2.30
Wootton Basset road	7. 0	Slough	—
Reading	8. 0	Wootton Basset road	4.30
Wootton Basset road	8.55	Maidenhead	—
(Mail Train.)		Wootton Basset road	6.30

Sunday Down Trains.		**Sunday Up Trains.**	
	h. m		h. m.
Wootton Basset road, A.M.	8. 0	Wootton Basset road, A.M.	2. 30
Slough	8.30	*(Mail Train.)*	
Reading	9. 0	Reading	—
Slough	9.30	Slough	—
Wootton Basset road, P.M.	2. 0	Wootton Basset road, P.M.	2. 0
Reading	5. 0	Slough	—
Slough	7. 0	Slough	—
Wootton Basset road	8.55	Wootton Basset road	5. 0
(Mail Train.)		Reading	—

Above left:

An early lithograph of the 'Biscuit Town' of Reading from the Thames. This shows many interesting features, including the tunnel connection to the H&P factory and both the Great Western and South Eastern lines. There is also what appears to be an early signal cabin (Kennet Bridge?) centre left.

T. Harden collection

Right:

On 17 December 1840 the Great Western line was opened through to Hay Lane (Wootton Bassett Road). This timetable of around the same date shows the new services. *B. Davis collection*

course of the line slightly to the south and instead form a cutting nearly two miles in length, at depths varying from 20ft-60ft. The contract for the section from Ruscombe to Reading was let out to a Mr William Ranger. Work commenced during the spring of 1836, and it appears that a tunnel under the Bath Road may still have been considered at this time. However, by 30 August 1838 with work well in hand, this proposal was abandoned when the directors decided on a road bridge at this point. The cutting bisected land that was extensively water-logged in places, the earth being mostly heavy clay,

sand and gravel, and just to move the spoil, which at the deepest point required the removal of 7,800cu ft per foot length, was a major engineering project in itself. Ranger and his navvies quite soon found the task beyond them, since the gravel made banking particularly difficult, and landslips were common. These resulted in many injuries and fatalities to the workers, and the work fell badly behind schedule. In order to speed things up the GWR removed Ranger from the contract and sub-let the work to three other contractors. These proved to be no better than the first, as once again the work fell behind schedule

Left:
The arrival of the railway brought much trade to the local hostelries. This advertisement for the nearby Railway Tavern dates from about 1841.
Author's collection

Right:
The memorial to Henry West in St Laurence's churchyard.
Author

when a particularly wet autumn turned the whole site into a quagmire. The delay was compounded when one of the contractors, called Knowles, who was working at the Reading end ran into financial trouble. This resulted in him being unable to pay his labourers, who immediately went on strike. Despite repeated requests from the Great Western for a resumption of work, nothing apparently happened, and Knowles was dismissed. A Great Western director called Gibbs rather understated the problem when he wrote after one visit, 'There appears to be a great deal to do at Sonning'. This second setback now left Brunel with no alternative but to take control of the work himself, and by February 1839 he had some 1,220 men and 196 horses employed on the excavation. This work was later supplemented by the use of two small locomotives, which were purchased to assist with the spoil removal; the resulting increase saw over 300,000cu ft per week of spoil being removed.

Accidents were still an almost daily occurrence: an interesting report from the *Reading Mercury* of July 1839 records the inadvertent explosion of a barrel of gunpowder which was being used to shift a vein of hardened clay. It seems that it injured five men, one of them being raised into the air for some distance, together with the truck he sat on. Two were taken to the nearby Royal Berks Hospital and the other three to their lodgings. The directors of the company were obviously mindful of the many injuries that the excavation was causing, for they donated 100 guineas plus an annual subscription of 10 guineas to the Royal Berks Hospital.

By the spring of 1839 there were still some 700,000cu yd of earth to be removed, but such was the progress that this had been completed by the end of the year. The deepest part of the cutting, which measured some 60ft, was crossed by two road bridges. The easterly bridge carried only a minor road and was at first constructed of timber. It was supported on four timber piers and had an overall span of some 240ft, and it survived until 1893 when it was replaced by an iron bridge. More spectacular, however, was the Bath Road bridge, which Brunel constructed of brick. Its three-arch span was also some 60ft high.

The great cutting at Sonning, perhaps with the exception of the tunnel at Box, was arguably the greatest piece of civil engineering undertaken on the route to Bristol. Much of the spoil from Sonning was used to raise the line above the flood plains of the River Kennet on the eastern approaches to Reading, and also to form several embankments at the Twyford end of the cutting. To cross the river on this section, Brunel constructed a 60ft span bridge built of brick, in a similar style to that at Maidenhead. Brunel had deliberately chosen to route the line close to the river here in order to follow it through the Goring gap. He did his job well, for the section from London to Reading and eventually to Didcot was built on the easy ruling gradient of 1 in 1,320 in the up direction, and no curve was of less than two miles radius. Although the line through Reading is of almost level gradient, the station, which stands on an embankment, is actually 143ft above the

Ordnance Datum. By 14 March 1840 the line was complete enough for a special train containing Brunel and a party of directors to make the run to Reading. Brunel himself travelled on the footplate of the locomotive *Evening Star* between Twyford and Reading, the journey from London taking just 70 minutes.

Because the town was situated to the south of the new line, Brunel rather ingeniously provided a one-sided station. It was built almost entirely of wood, the up and down platforms were in effect two separate stations, built end-to-end but a short distance apart. The up platform was situated at the London end, and the whole structure was covered by a zinc roof, supported by rows of iron columns.

At about 3.30pm on 24 March, only six days before it was opened to the public, a bizarre accident took place at Reading station. Severe weather conditions saw a particularly strong gust of wind lift part of the roof from the main train shed. Unfortunately a 24-year old journeyman carpenter by the name of Henry West was working on the roof at the time. It seems that he, together with a four ton glazed section of the roof, were carried some 200ft before eventually crashing to the ground, killing him instantly. His body was recovered and taken to the Boar's Head Inn at Friar Street to await the coroner's inquest, which was performed the same evening. His funeral took place at St Laurence's churchyard on the following Sunday, and over 40 of his working colleagues apparently turned up to pay their last respects. A memorial board in St Laurence's church-yard is still *in situ* today and records that 'he lost his life in a whirlwind'.

On 28 March the Gooch 7ft Single *Fire Fly* hauling a short train containing about 40 directors and guests, covered the 35¾ miles from Paddington to Reading in only 45 minutes. Duly satisfied, the Great Western Railway proudly announced that on and after Monday 30 March 1840, the line between London and Reading would be open to convey

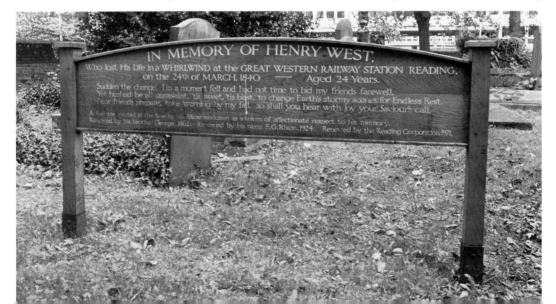

passengers, carriages, horses, goods and parcels. Thousands of people flocked to the lineside to witness the first train, the 6.00am to Paddington, hauled by the locomotive *Firefly*. Newspaper reports state that some 17 trains arrived and departed on that first day, and that Forbury Hill, which commanded a good view of the approaching trains, was crowded with sightseers. Third class passengers, described by the Great Western as 'persons of the lower station of life', had not been carried by the company until the line had reached Reading, and only then in open wagons tagged on to the back of a goods train. It was to one of these trains that befell the first major accident on the railway near Reading. This occurred on the morning of Christmas Eve 1841 when the 4.30am down goods ran into a land-slip, which had occurred towards the centre of Sonning Cutting. The locomotive *Hecla*, a 2-4-0 of the 'Leo' class, built by Fenton, Murray & Jackson of Leeds

during April of that year, together with two third class carriages and 18 goods wagons, was derailed. The two passenger vehicles containing some 38 travellers were unfortunately crushed by the force of the goods wagons. In all eight persons were killed and 17 seriously injured; the crash was made all the worse because at this time vehicles were not fitted with spring buffers. It seems that the train was unusually full, with many of the extra travellers workmen who were engaged on building the new Houses of Parliament, travelling home for Christmas. Incidentally the very first fixed signal to be used on the new railway appears to have been installed at Reading, as Gooch's *Regulations for the engines working the trains on and after 30 March 1840* states 'A signal ball will be seen at the entrance to Reading station when the line is right for the train to go in. If the ball is not visible the train must not pass it'.

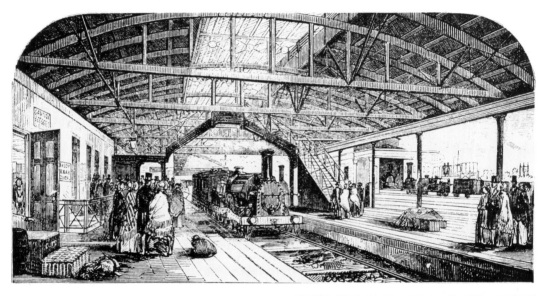

Above:
This Measom drawing depicts the locomotive *Hero* arriving at the up station at Reading in 1852. The broad gauge locomotive shed is also shown, in the right background. *Author's collection*

Right:
This view shows the entrance to the up station at Reading circa 1860. *Author's collection*

The arrival of the Great Western Railway at Reading certainly sounded the death knell for canal traffic, and by 1841, with the line extended through to Bristol the canal company's receipts for that year had plummeted by some 50%, caused when almost the entire through traffic between London and Bristol was switched to the new railway, although it must be said that local traffic continued to use the canal for many years. Other casualties of the new railway were the many stage coach services which by 1844 had ceased to run between Reading and London. During the same year the GWR Hotel was opened at Reading. It was apparently designed by Brunel himself and its opening ensured a further decline in the use of the old coaching inns. In 1852 the canal company was purchased by the Great Western, who in 1867 converted all of the K&ACC shares into railway stock. Although the new railway effectively killed off the canal, it helped not only in bringing many new firms to the town, but also in the expansion of some existing ones, notably the well known biscuit manufacturers Huntley & Palmers and the seed growers Suttons. Huntley & Palmers had started with a staff of just four and by the turn of the century were the world's largest biscuit manufacturers, employing some 6,000 people. I have described Huntley & Palmers in greater detail in a later chapter, but this interesting little rhyme aptly sums up H&P's importance to the town of Reading:

On the banks of Kennet's River
In Reading's famous town
Stands a massive pile of Buildings
Of fame and world renown.

Should a stranger ask the business
Of the place what may it be?
Say 'tis the biscuit city
Of the famous H&P.

Another local company whose success could be directly linked to the coming of the railway was Suttons Seeds. Martin Hope Sutton started his seed and bulb merchant's business in 1837. His father John Sutton had himself previously traded at Market Place, Reading as a corn and seed merchant from about 1806, and he joined his son in the new venture. The premises at Market Place became the company's headquarters, and were extended during 1872-73 to cover an area of eventually some 5 acres. It was around this same date that Suttons set up extensive trial grounds, covering an area of some 60 acres, which bordered the south side of the Great Western main line to the east of Reading station, seasonally employing over 700 people. The firm became famous for the purity of its seeds, selling its products world-wide. They were also quick to see the potential of the railway, which they soon exploited after the advent of the penny post in 1840 by sending many of their products, on a carriage-free basis, by rail throughout the country.

In a smaller way Reading was also known for its ale. In 1700 some 104 inns supplied the population of 8,000 and by 1846 there were some 21 breweries in the town, probably the best known and longest surviving was W. B. Simonds (absorbed into the Courage group during 1960). William Blackall Simonds opened his first brewery in Broad Street in 1785, moving to new larger premises in Bridge Street in 1790. For many years during this century the brewery had its own railway connection via the Great Western Coley goods branch. Thus over the years Reading became a town of three Bs: Beer,

Above:
This lithograph shows the Reading biscuit factory in about 1890. *T. Harden collection*

Biscuits and Bulbs. It is worth mentioning another major employer who arrived at Reading around the same time as the railway. This was the Reading Iron Co, which by 1869 was employing some 400 men at its Kates Grove works on the production of both portable engines and fixed mills.

The next stage in the growth of the Great Western at Reading came in 1845 with the sanctioning by parliament of the Berks & Hants line. The contract was let for the whole of the line in one go, and by August 1847 Brunel was able to report that the work was 'all but completed'. The line was obviously well engineered as Brunel acknowledged 'that the circumstances of its becoming in all probability the main line to the West of England has been attended to'. The first 25½ mile broad gauge section between Reading and a temporary terminus at Hungerford was opened for passenger traffic on 21 December 1847, and unusually, to goods a year later. The temporary station at Hungerford was to allow for the projected extension to Westbury, and was built to the same one-sided principle as used by Brunel at Reading. Intermediate stations on the line were provided at Theale, Aldermaston, Woolhampton (which was renamed Midgham in 1873), Thatcham, Newbury and Kintbury, and a further station at Reading West was opened in July 1906.

The second portion of this branch, to Basingstoke, left the Hungerford line via Southcote Junction. The building of the line was delayed somewhat due to the hostile nature of the LSWR, who wanted assurances as to both the position of the GW terminus and methods of communication between here and their own station nearby. At this time a junction between the Basingstoke branch and the LSWR main line was not possible, due to the change in gauge. Eventually the problems between the two companies were partially resolved and the 13½ mile broad gauge Basingstoke branch was opened for traffic on 1 November 1848. The LSWR still remained hostile to this GW incursion into its territory, and for many years Great Western passenger trains were confined to the Great Western station only at Basingstoke. For the opening of the line one intermediate station was provided, at Mortimer, and a second station was subsequently opened at Bramley in April 1895. The GWR passenger station at Basingstoke survived until 1 January 1932, after which date it was closed and services were diverted into the ex-LSWR station.

Brunel's broad gauge supremacy at Reading was to take a knock with the opening, on 22 December 1856, of mixed gauge lines from Oxford southwards through to Basingstoke. The mixing of the gauges over this route had been authorised by an Act of Parliament of 31 July 1854. To gain access to the Basingstoke branch required the building of a new

Above:

Mortimer station, on the Reading-Basingstoke branch was opened on 1 November 1848. This interesting picture, taken around the turn of the century, shows possibly the whole of the station staff.
Author's collection

Below:

The Great Western station at Reading circa 1849.

loop line to the west of Reading via two new junctions at Oxford Road and Reading West. Once opened, standard gauge goods services were inaugurated between Basingstoke and Wolverhampton, the first standard gauge service over the new route being composed of general goods and coal traffic. The mixing of the gauges continued and on 1 October 1861 they were opened between Reading West

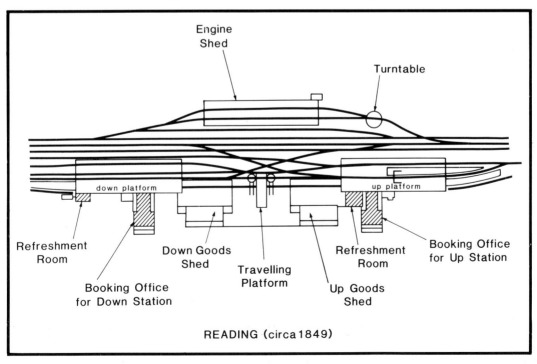

Engine Shed

Turntable

down platform

up platform

Refreshment Room

Booking Office for Down Station

Down Goods Shed

Travelling Platform

Refreshment Room

Up Goods Shed

Booking Office for Up Station

READING (circa 1849)

Junction and Paddington, a distance of 36 miles 78 chains. The passenger service was inaugurated on the same day with three through trains to and from Birkenhead and Wolverhampton. The first service was the 9.35 to Birkenhead, and all initially stopped at Reading. This, however, was not the first standard gauge line to be opened by the Great Western to the east of Reading, as that honour fell to the short single-line connection between the South Eastern and the Great Western that was opened on 1 December 1858. The building of this line by the Great Western was caused by the Staines, Wokingham & Reading company, who under the umbrella of the LSWR, had running powers to enter Reading via SER lines. In 1857 this small company had gained royal assent to build a standard gauge connection from the SER route at Reading and to connect with the mixed gauge track between Reading and Tilehurst. One of the conditions of this proposal was that this could only go ahead providing the GWR did not within one year make its own standard gauge connection to the SER line at Reading. In order to stop the Staines company's incursion into its territory, the GW duly completed a 1½ mile standard gauge connection to the SE line. This ran from the Reading West Junction past

GREAT WESTERN RAILWAY.

Maiden Erlegh Steeplechases,

WEDNESDAY and THURSDAY,

November 15th & 16th, 1905.

ON THE ABOVE DATES

Cheap Tickets

WILL BE ISSUED TO

READING

From	By Trains as under		Return Fares.			From	By Trains as under		Return Fares.		
			1st Class.	2nd Class.	3rd Class.				1st Class.	2nd Class.	3rd Class.
	A.M.	A.M.	s. d.	s. d.	s. d.		A.M.	NOON	s. d.	s. d.	s. d.
Swindon	9 15	10 50	8 9	5 5	4 4	Culham	9 53	11 53	4 2	2 6	2 1
Shrivenham	9 25	12 0	7 6	4 9	3 9	Didcot	10 24	12 5	3 7	2 4	1 10
Faringdon	9 22	12 0	7 3	4 7	3 8	Wallingford	10 20	12 2	3 2	2 0	1 7
Uffington	9 38	12 13	6 3	4 1	3 3	Chols'y&Moulsf'd	10 34	12 16	2 6	1 8	1 4
						Goring&Streatley	10 43	12 26	1 11	1 3	1 0
Challow	9 46	12 21	5 10	3 9	2 11	Newbury	10 33	11 39	3 7	2 4	1 10
Wantage Road	9 56	12 31	5 0	3 2	2 7	Thatcham	9 25	11 57	2 10	1 10	1 5
Steventon	10 8	12 42	4 5	2 9	2 2	Midgham	9 31	12 3	2 3	1 6	1 2
		A.M.				Aldermaston	9 37	12 9	1 11	1 3	1 0
Oxford	9 35	11 35	5 8	3 9	2 11	Basingstoke	10 5	11 45	3 2	2 1	1 8
Abingdon	9 30	11 12	5 3	3 4	2 8	Bramley	10 15	11 56	2 3	1 6	1 2
Radley	9 46	11 46	4 9	3 2	2 5	Mortimer	10 23	12 3	1 6	1 2	1 0

The Tickets will be available for return from Reading by any train after 4.0 p.m. on the day of issue only

Children under Three years of age, Free ; Three and under Twelve, Half-Price.

THE TICKETS ARE NOT TRANSFERABLE.

NO LUGGAGE ALLOWED.

Should an Excursion or Cheap Ticket be used for any other Station than those named upon it, or by any other Train than as above specified, it will be rendered void, and therefore the Fare paid will be liable to forfeiture, and the full Ordinary Fare will become chargeable.

PADDINGTON, November, 1905. **JAMES C. INGLIS, General Manager.**

L.D. 277. 1,000. WYMAN & SONS, LTD, Printers, Fetter Lane, London, E.C., and Reading.—2374a.
B.D. 300.

Reading station and via a low level tunnel under the GW main line to connect with the SER line to the east of Reading. Although the line was completed within the time limit, it did not open for traffic until 1 December 1858, to allow for some exchange sidings to be completed at the lower level. What seemed to the GWR at first to be a relatively unimportant connection, soon became an important through link between the Midlands and the Channel ports. In 1859 the Great Western signal works were established at Reading. These lay on the North (Caversham) side of the line and adjacent to the station, and are described in detail in a later chapter.

On 11 November 1862 the Berks & Hants line was extended from Hungerford to Devizes, not by the earlier company but by the newly formed Berks & Hants Extension Railway, and it remained independent until absorbed by the GW in 1882. On 13 June 1865 the town clerk of Reading wrote a letter to the Great Western offering both land and support to the company to site the proposed carriage works at Reading. Competition was rife, with other towns and cities such as Abingdon, Gloucester, and Oxford also showing great interest in having the works, which of course were eventually sited at Swindon.

The gradual mixing of the gauge continued, but Reading station itself was not mixed until April 1869, partly due to the complexity of the trackwork required over the one-sided layout. In fact until this time passengers were forced to use a pair of temporary open platforms to embark and disembark from the standard gauge services. Mixed gauge services were spreading rapidly throughout the system and by the late 1870s the only regular broad gauge workings passing through Reading were to the South-west. In 1880 the old broad gauge locomotive shed was closed and replaced by a new standard gauge shed to the west of the station. The population was now expanding rapidly, particularly to the west of Reading, and in order to serve this new area of population, the Great Western opened during

1882, a new station 2½ miles west of Reading at Tilehurst. Tilehurst officially became part of Reading when the town boundary was extended westwards in 1911.

Broad gauge services finally came to an end on Friday 20 May 1892, the last broad gauge service to pass through Reading being the up 'Night Mail' which arrived at Paddington on Saturday 21 May at 5.30am, some 1½hr late. The removal of the broad gauge now allowed various track improvements to take place, with the quadrupling of the lines between Taplow and Didcot. At Sonning Cutting the extra space needed was achieved by cutting back the edges, building retaining walls and reducing the depth of the cutting, thus giving a wider trackbed. The work also involved much bridge widening in the Reading area, and by 4 June 1893 the quadrupling had reached to the east end of Reading station. The section from Reading West Junction to Pangbourne was opened on 30 July of the same year. The Great Western now had a four track layout from Paddington right through to Didcot, except interestingly for a 1½ mile section through Reading station yard. Macdermot states that the quadrupling of this last section was not completed until 1899. But as the two new relief platforms at Reading were opened on 2 May 1898, it seems reasonable to assume that the quadrupling of this final section had been completed by this date. On 17 December 1899 a new junction was opened between the South Eastern and Great Western lines to the east of the station. This junction now allowed for a much greater flexibility for through inter-company working than the old 1858 connection. New goods loops were installed between the East End box and Scours Lane, together with a new double line for the use of all goods trains running to West Junction sorting sidings.

A new goods station, together with coal and mileage yards, also opened to the north and east of Reading station in June 1896. These new yards

replaced the earlier goods depot that was swept away to make room for the new station. On 1 July 1906 a new interchange station was opened at Reading West. On the following day the Great Western finally opened the last link, between Castle Cary and Cogland Junction, of the Berks & Hants route to Taunton. Almost immediately many of the through services to the South-west were switched away from the longer Bristol route. In order to speed up these services, between November 1911 and February 1912 considerable work was undertaken on the relaying of the Berks & Hants Junction to the west of Reading station. The resulting alterations, which saw the turn out curves flattened from 15 to 30 chains radius, raised the junction speed from 20 to 40mph. Probably the last major development in the growth of the railway at Reading was the opening on 4 May 1908 of the 1¾ mile-long Coley goods branch and the new 'Central goods depot'.

The South Eastern and the London & South Western

The South Eastern Railway was incorporated in 1836 with authority to construct a line from a junction with the London & Croydon Railway at Norwood through to Dover, via Oxted, Tonbridge and Ashford. It was opened to passengers as far as Tonbridge on 26 May 1842 and extended through to Dover on 7 February 1844. A clause in the Act had decreed that to avoid a duplication of lines out of London, the South Eastern should jointly share the construction costs of about 20 miles of the route with the London & Brighton Railway, with whom it would have joint running powers as far as Reigate Junction. Work was started by the London & Brighton in 1839, with the line being opened to passengers as far as Haywards Heath on 12 July 1841 and to Brighton on 21 September of the same year. At Redstone Hill (Reigate Junction) the two routes diverged. At this time the future town of Redhill was mostly green fields with just a few houses, known locally as Warwick town. In order to gain traffic from the nearby town of Reigate both the London & Brighton and the South Eastern companies had built their own separate stations approximately ½-mile apart. The London & Brighton station stood to the south of the junction, and was opened on 12 July 1841. The South Eastern station lay much more conveniently, just to the north of the junction, and opened almost a year later on 26 May 1842. The establishment of two stations so close together was particularly inconvenient for the passengers, as apparently the London & Brighton was refusing to stop at the SE station. Eventually common sense prevailed and on 6 May 1844 the LBSCR station was closed. Thereafter its trains called at the South Eastern station, thereby establishing Reigate Junction (Redhill) firmly on the railway map.

Once the line to Dover was open, various schemes were proposed to extend the railway westwards from the junction at Reigate. The company that succeeded in gaining both finance and parliamentary approval to do so was the Reading, Guildford & Reigate Railway. This company was incorporated on 16 July 1846, to construct a line

Above:
This engraving is of the first South Eastern station at Forbury. It shows to good effect the overall roof and the simple entrance building. In the background is the Great Western station. Notice also the wooden viaduct over the Vastern Road, and the large disc and crossbar signal. *B. Davis collection*

some 45 miles in length between Reigate Junction (Redhill) on the London & Brighton Railway and Reading on the Great Western. The company was initially promoted by an alliance of Surrey bankers and businessmen, with more than a little support from the South Eastern, which probably saw this as a possible through link between the Channel ports and the Midlands.

The line was gradually opened in various stages from each end, firstly with the simultaneous completion on 4 July 1849 of the 16½-mile northern section from Reading to Farnborough, and the 8-mile southern section between Redhill and Dorking. The line was again extended with the opening of the section between Farnborough and Ash Junction on 20 August 1849. This was actually the final contract to be let, and was awarded to a Mr G. Furness at a cost of £17,796. From Ash Junction the line joined the LSWR Alton branch, over which running powers were exercised in order to reach Guildford. The station here, on the London & South Western's line to Woking, had been opened by the LSWR in 1845. Through running between Reading and Redhill became possible on 15 October 1849 with the completion by the LSWR of the final section between Guildford and Shalford Junction. The SER who had backed the line from the start reached agreement with the RG&RR on 16 July 1846 to both lease and work the line at a cost of 4½% of the gross receipts plus half the surplus profits. Eventually this was modified to a single payment of 5% of the gross receipts. This method of working the line continued until 1852 when under the Act of 19 June, the Reading, Guildford & Reigate company was purchased outright by the South Eastern. It appears that the South Eastern shareholders were somewhat unhappy at this action, with many accusing the then Chairman, John MacGregor, of paying an excessive price. The financial arguments

continued until MacGregor himself resigned in 1854. Under a separate agreement the SER was also paying the LSWR some 35% of its gross receipts for running rights over its sections. This was not a very satisfactory state of affairs, and to try to reduce this payment, the SER had in September 1851 introduced for a short time a free horse-drawn omnibus service between Guildford and Shalford. This, of course, did not enhance the working relationship between the two companies and it was to take several more years before peace finally prevailed. For the opening of the line the South Eastern provided a service of four trains a day in each direction, running alternately to Tonbridge and Reigate. During 1852 the timetable from Reading was supplemented with the addition of a new express service to London Bridge. Leaving Reading at 8.45am and calling at Guildford, Shalford and Dorking, it reached London Bridge at 10.45am. The down service left London at 6.00pm calling at Redhill instead of Dorking. The following year the fast service was increased to three up and two down trains daily. Incidentally a through service to London Bridge survived right up until the end of steam traction in 1965 in the form of the 7.27am Reading-London Bridge and the 5.25pm return service. Accidents on this line have been few and far between, but what was possibly the first occurred on Wednesday 12 September 1855 when locomotive No 96, a long boilered 0-6-0 built by Nasmyth & Gaskell in 1844, was despatched from Reading accidentally on the down line. Approximately one mile from the station it collided head-on with the 4.40pm service from London Bridge to Reading, hauled by No 7, a Hick-built 2-4-0.

Below:
The South Eastern station at Forbury circa 1850.

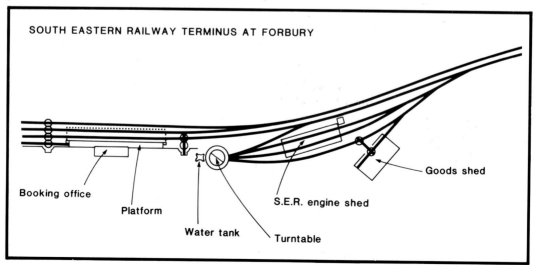

SOUTH EASTERN RAILWAY TERMINUS AT FORBURY

Booking office

Platform

Water tank

Turntable

S.E.R. engine shed

Goods shed

Above:

Entitled *Reading from the Line*, this Measom drawing shows the South Eastern station at Reading (right) and also, more importantly, the original two-road South Eastern engine shed (right centre). The other building is the South Eastern goods shed. On the left is St Laurence's Church and Reading Gaol.

Author's collection

Unfortunately the driver of No 96 was killed on the spot along with four passengers, 10 others were seriously injured, three of whom later died in the Royal Berks Hospital.

The LSWR, under the auspices of the Staines, Wokingham & Woking Junction Railway, had reached Reading during 1856 with the opening on 9 July of through services between Reading and Waterloo. The completion of this route became possible firstly with the opening by the Richmond & West End Railway of its line between Battersea (Clapham Junction) and Richmond on 27 July 1846. This company was purchased by the LSWR during the following year. On 22 August 1848 the line was extended through to Staines, by the LSWR under the auspices of the Windsor, Staines & South Western Railway. In 1852 yet another LSWR-backed company, the Staines, Wokingham & Woking Junction Railway was formed to extend the line through to Wokingham. Tenders for the construction of the track over this section were let to McCormicks, and the station and ancillary buildings to the firm of Oades & Sons. Interestingly in 1845 the possible construction of a line between Staines and Wokingham had been the subject of proposals by no fewer than six different companies.

On 12 July 1858 an agreement had been reached between the SW&WJR and the LSWR that the latter company would lease the line from the former for a period of 42 years. However, this arrangement was to last for only 20 years, for in 1878 the SW&WR was absorbed by the LSWR. The first section between Staines and Ascot was opened on 4 June 1856, and finally connected with the SER route to Reading at Wokingham on 9 July of the same year. Agreement had been reached between the two companies as to joint working over the final 6¾-mile section into Reading. It appears that the initial fares over the route were rather high, as this report from the *Reading Mercury* of 12 July points out:

'On Wednesday morning this line was opened, but the carriages went off with some very light loads; this, we apprehend, may be attributable to the scale of fares, which, as regards the transit from Reading to London exceeds that of the Great Western and nearly doubles that of the South Eastern. It is true that the distance from Reading to Waterloo Bridge is accomplished in rather under two hours, which may be great accommodation to some, as the tedious omnibus travelling is avoided from Paddington to the Strand.'

For the opening of the line an hourly service was provided between Reading and Waterloo. It is worth recording at this point that a proposal had been made by the SW&WJR to extend its line right through to Oxford, where it could connect with the standard gauge Oxford, Worcester & Wolverhampton Railway. The thought of a North-South standard gauge route was tempting, but this proposal along with other similar ones by the same company was eventually abandoned.

Very soon after the South Eastern had reached Reading its thoughts turned to the lucrative London traffic. The GWR had the advantage of the shorter route (36 miles), the LSWR route to Waterloo was 43½ miles, whereas the South Eastern route via Redhill to Charing Cross was 68¾ miles. Apart from this obvious disadvantage, its trains had gained a reputation for being slow, dirty and unpunctual. The only way it seemed that the South Eastern could compete with the other companies was by reducing its fares between Reading and London. Unfortunately each reduction was almost immediately matched by both the Great Western and the LSWR, and this resulted in a fare war that ended up with absurdly low fares on all three routes, which of course delighted the customers but not the share-

Above:
The rebuilt South Eastern station at Reading around 1870. The rather overpowering Great Western station can be seen on the right. *Pamlin Prints*

holders. This ridiculous state of affairs could quite obviously not continue, and eventually in June 1858 an agreement regarding the charging of both equal fares and a fairer distribution of receipts was signed by all parties. This was a rather strange agreement for it involved a pooling of the fares, with the Great Western taking a two-thirds cut of the combined passenger revenues of the three companies, and the South Eastern and the London & South Western taking a two-thirds share of the combined revenue from the goods traffic. The agreement also put an end to the fast through services to London Bridge that had been inaugurated by the South Eastern in 1852. At Reading the line terminated at a small single platform station at North Forbury Road. The platform measured approximately 180ft in length and wagon turntables appear to have been provided at either end. An overall roof 190ft long by 41ft wide covered both the single platform and a siding which was probably used for carriage storage. To the east of the station stood a goods shed, together with a small single road locomotive shed, behind which was situated a 45ft turntable.

This first 'temporary' station did not last very long, for during 1854 proposals were submitted to construct a brand new terminus. This was to be situated on the west side of Vastern Road, which would be crossed by a newly-constructed bridge. Work was started in March 1855 and progressed well, with the new station being finished and ready for use on 30 August 1855. The new terminus was in a far more convenient position, standing almost alongside the Great Western station. This second station was constructed of wood and contained a

double-sided platform that measured approximately 350ft in length, the two faces being partially covered at the western end by a 150ft×40ft overall roof. This, however, had an even shorter life than the old station, since on Sunday 26 June 1859 it was apparently struck by lightning during a fierce storm. This resulted in a fire that severely damaged much of the wooden structure. The subsequent rebuilding work gave the company an opportunity to improve the facilities, the work being completed during the summer of 1860. The new station now had a new longer platform (400ft) but the biggest improvement of all was a new station entrance building. This was built of brick and was altogether a much more substantial affair. The two-storey building contained on the ground floor, waiting rooms together with a large entrance lobby and ticket office; situated above these were other offices for the administration staff. In 1857 both the South Eastern and the Staines, Wokingham & Woking Junction had deposited separate Bills for a standard gauge line from Reading to Tilehurst, where a connection would be made with the mixed gauge route from Basingstoke to the Midlands. The South Eastern proposal was for a line which ran to the south of the Great Western station, joining the standard gauge rails near Reading West Junction. With Great Western opposition the South Eastern Bill was rejected, but on 27 July 1857 the SW&WJ Bill was passed with the unusual condition that the company would be compelled to lay the line, unless within one year the GWR undertook the work themselves. A subsequent agreement between the two companies saw the Great Western undertake the work. This comprised a single standard gauge line from Reading West Junction to connect with the lower level SW&WJ route to Wokingham via a short skew tunnel under the GW main line. This connection, known as the Reading Junction Line, should have opened on 1 September 1858 but was delayed when it was decided to double the track. It was eventually completed and opened for goods on 1 December 1858 and to passengers on 17 January 1859. The SER, on payment of a toll, was also granted running rights over the line. During 1896 work was started on further improvements to the station and by

26 December of the same year a second platform had been added, thus increasing the number from two to four. The overall roof was also removed and replaced with individual platform awnings, but the main entrance block which had been constructed after the 1859 fire was retained. In order to accommodate the extra platforms the Vastern Road bridge was widened to take four tracks. This required the removal of the old brick arch and its replacement with a new iron girder structure. Other improvements saw additional sidings constructed in

Below:
Drummond 'M7' class 0-4-4T No 30026 awaits departure from Platform 1 at Reading South with a service to Waterloo on 16 April 1953. *V. R. Webster*

both the station and goods yard, the small goods shed was enlarged and the offices rebuilt. A new signalbox was constructed adjacent to the station, the work being finally finished on 1 January 1898.

One year later on 1 January 1899 the South Eastern was amalgamated into the South Eastern & Chatham Railway, and during the same year an additional double track connection from the low level SECR lines to the higher level Great Western was opened on 17 December. This was soon used by the through passenger services between the Midlands and the South-east that had been inaugurated during 1897 and had previously used the old 1858 connection. It is interesting to reflect, that at this time the South Eastern and the LSWR each maintained their own separate booking and goods offices, each of course manned with the individual company's own staff. It seems, however, that the uniformed platform staff were provided solely by the South Eastern Railway, which also performed all the outside work such as shunting and train forming. The total number of staff employed on the 'Southern' side of Reading at this time was about 250. By the turn of the century the whole of the southern complex at Reading was controlled by three signalboxes. Reading Junction box was opened during 1898 and was a direct replacement for an earlier box which stood on the same site. On opening it was fitted with a 125-lever frame but some time

between the wars this was replaced with a smaller 66-lever frame, which it retained until closure on 5 September 1965. Reading Station box, as already mentioned, opened in 1898 and again replaced an earlier box that had stood on a slightly different site. The new box opened with a 75-lever frame but apparently during 1909 this was shortened to 65; it also was closed on 5 September 1965. Early maps also show a third box, at Reading Gas Siding, but ex Reading shedmaster Jack Hewett confirms that this was no more than a covered ground frame released from the nearby Junction box. It was probably installed shortly after the opening of the gas works in 1872, and it lasted until 9 November 1932, after which it was removed during track alterations in the yard. The goods yard here was very busy with about eight freight services, comprising intermediate and fast freights to and from the yards at Feltham, Guildford and Redhill in and out of the yard daily.

A feature of the goods service for a number of years was the nightly through van train to Bricklayers Arms. Stations on the LSWR line between Reading and Ascot were served by an afternoon pick-up goods. A second pick-up goods served the intermediate stations on the South Eastern route to Guildford. This line was also served by an early evening roadbox train which called at Crowthorne, Blackwater, Farnborough North and North Camp with supplies, which it seems included

Above left:

This view, taken from Main Line East Box shows, from left to right, the GW main line, the 1899 Incline Junction and the Southern locomotive shed.

B. Davis collection

Right:

This LSWR poster, dated 16 August 1892, advertises a special excursion to the Crystal Palace from Reading South.

G. A. Carpenter collection

a considerable amount of beer for the various military establishments in the area. If there is such a thing as a crack freight, then at Reading it must have been the 7.15pm fast to Feltham. Known locally by Southern men as the 'Biscuit', it was timed to reach Feltham in just one hour, to connect with the fast service to Southampton. By the 1930s passenger services from Reading comprised an hourly service to Waterloo and about 20 services daily in each direction to Guildford, Redhill and Tonbridge. During the summer months many excursions were run to such destinations as Hastings, Canterbury, Folkestone, Margate and Ramsgate. Also for many years extra trains were run from Reading in connection with the races at Royal Ascot, and on Gold Cup day in particular, it seems that the regular passenger service was suspended and replaced with special race trains. Race specials were also run in the other direction from Ascot to the races at Newbury, with an LSWR engine working right through. In 1938 Great Western motive power became a regular feature on the line when Churchward 2-6-0s were rostered to work the 6.15am service from Reading through to Redhill, returning on the 10.17am. This became a long-running feature of services on the line, with the

Moguls being joined in later years by examples of the GW 'Manor' class.

On 1 January 1939 the inauguration of a new electric service between Reading and Waterloo was made possible by conversion to the Southern Electric third rail system of the 20½-miles of track between Virginia Water, Ascot and Reading.

The first electric trains ran on the LBSR between Victoria and London Bridge from 1 December 1909. This early service, which used the overhead system, was extended to Crystal Palace some two years later. The first third rail route was opened on 25 August 1915 and ran between Waterloo and East Putney. After the Grouping in 1923, the newly formed Southern Railway pressed ahead with third rail electrification. The first main line to be converted was the ex-LBSR route between London, Brighton and Worthing. Conversion was started during 1929 and eventually cost some £22,750,000. Such was the success of electrification that by 1935 all the suburban lines between Gravesend and Sevenoaks on the Eastern Section, and Guildford and Windsor on the Western Section had been converted. During the same year a new programme was announced to continue the electrification of the outer suburban system as far as Reading, and at the same time to complete some smaller sections in the Aldershot and Guildford areas. A total of 43 route miles were

Far left:
A Drummond 'K10' class 4-4-0 stands in the Southern station at Reading with a service to Waterloo, on 5 June 1930.
OURS collection

Far left below:
Ex-Great Western Mogul No 6379 leaves Reading South with the 6.50am service to Redhill.
Author's collection

Left:
Timetable announcing the new electric services to Waterloo.
B. Davis collection

converted at a total cost of some £1,000,000. The final section of the newly converted route, from Wokingham to Reading, was officially energised on 24 October 1938. The formal opening took place on Friday 30 December 1938. Services commenced on 1 January 1939, with 36 through trains daily in each direction between Waterloo, Ascot, Wokingham and Reading replacing 20 steam services, the average journey time being cut by 11min. The new trains gave a half-hourly service throughout the day,

leaving Reading at 19 and 59 minutes past the hour. In the down direction the service was usually formed of two four-car sets; these split at Ascot, with one section going to Reading, the other to Camberley and Aldershot. In order to operate the service 36 new 2-BIL units Nos 2117-2152 were constructed during 1938/39. To accommodate the new trains, platforms 3 and 4 at Reading were electrified, together with a pair of unit stabling roads alongside platform 4. At the same time a new

booking office, built in brick, was constructed alongside the existing station building. Eventually all four platform lines were energised. The general pattern of working which evolved saw the electric services use platform 4, Redhill trains platform 3, with 1 and 2 being used mainly for parcels and empty stock. World War 2 saw the construction of an additional connection between what was now the Southern Railway and the Great Western approximately ¾-mile to the east of Reading. The original 1899 connection was poorly situated, contained a gradient of 1 in 64 in the down direction and, worst

of all, did not give direct access to the goods avoiding lines through Reading, the latter point being essential for the rapidly increasing wartime traffic. The new connection known as the East Spur, was opened on 16 March 1941. The double track junction from the Southern line together with two pairs of loops and sidings were controlled by a newly constructed East Spur Junction signalbox. Built of brick and concrete, it contained 32 levers. To avoid building a second new box at the Great Western end of the junction a small miniature lever power frame with all electric interlocking was installed in Reading Main Line East box. On 1 January 1948 the Southern Railway became part of British Railways, with seemingly little immediate change locally. However, on 26 September 1949 the station was officially renamed Reading South, and this lasted until 11 September 1961 when the station was renamed Reading Southern.

On 4 January 1965 the remaining scheduled steam-hauled passenger services between Reading South and Guildford ceased and were replaced with a full diesel-operated timetable. At the same time all services between Reading and Tonbridge were downgraded to second class only. Six sets of three-car 'Tadpole' units, Nos 1201-1206 were made up at Eastleigh works during 1964 for the new services. The sets were formed of power and trailer cars from Hastings diesel units Nos 1002/3/4 together with the driving trailers from 2-EPB units Nos 5701/4/8/9/10/11.

The very last official steam-hauled passenger service, the 10.40pm service to Guildford left Reading on the evening of Sunday 3 January 1965 hauled by Maunsell 'U' class No 31809. On the same day the LCGB 'Maunsell Commemorative Railtour' visited Reading hauled in the down direction by 'Q' class No 30545 and outwards by 'N' class 2-6-0 No 31831, driven by the longest-serving member of the footplate staff at Reading, Driver Ralph Powell. Luckily for the enthusiast, diesel failures on the passenger services saw steam-hauled substitutes continue at Reading almost until the end of the year.

In March the management of the station was transferred to the Western Region and at the same time it was announced that the Southern station would be closed and services diverted into a new platform at Reading General. The total cost of the operation was put at £250,000. In preparation for this, the 1899 connection was closed to traffic from

Left:
The exterior of the ex-South Eastern station, pictured here in the early 1960s. The building dates from 1860, although the travel bureau was added in 1939, and enlarged in 1954. *Lens of Sutton*

Below left:
Race specials formed of 4-COR No 3134 and 4-RES No 3072 at Reading during Ascot week, 1965. The third unit, 2-BIL No 2098, is on the regular Waterloo service. *B. Davis collection*

Below:
The entrance to the platforms at Reading Southern, pictured here on 3 September 1965 just a couple of days before its closure. The various notices are announcing that from Monday 6 September services will leave from the adjacent General station. *C. Haydon*

Left:
Maunsell 'Q' class 0-6-0 No 30545 arrives at Reading on Sunday 3 January 1965 with the 'Maunsell Commemorative Railtour'. This was the last day of official steam passenger operation from Reading South. *D. Tuck*

Below left:
'N' class No 31831 prepares to take the return leg of the 'Maunsell Commemorative Railtour' from Reading on 3 January 1965. *D. Tuck*

Above:
2-HAL No 2677 approaches Reading on the newly electrified incline junction with a service from Waterloo in January 1966. Reading Junction signalbox can just be seen behind the unit. *G. A. Carpenter collection*

Below:
The remains of the Southern station, seen here in use as a service station circa 1975. *C. Haydon*

4 April to allow the trackwork to be remodelled and converted to third rail electric power. The very last service from Reading South left for Redhill from platform 2 at 11.24pm on Saturday 4 September 1965 hauled by Type 3 diesel No D6583. On Sunday 5 September the engineers were given complete occupation of the line between Reading and Wokingham for both track alterations and resignalling work, and from Monday 6 September, Southern Region services were transferred into the new bay platform (4A) at Reading General. The Southern station, which was closed on the same day, was subsequently taken over by Gowrings and saw further use as a garage, with the station yard being used as a car park for the nearby Western Region station. Although capable of holding eight coaches, it was asking rather a lot to expect that the one single platform provided here should be able to accommodate both the diesel services to Redhill and

Right:
The undulating nature of the east incline is shown to good effect as Class 206 unit No 1206 arrives at Reading with the 11.51 service from Tonbridge on 1 August 1980. *J. E. Oxley*

Bottom:
The final removal of the Southern station took place during August 1982. In this view the demolition is almost complete. *C. Haydon*

the electric services to Waterloo, which at peak times are strengthened to eight coaches. Quite often heavy delays were experienced when one service had to wait for the other to clear the platform, so for many years a good number of the Redhill trains were diverted into the other platforms at Reading. However, to coincide with the promotion of new through services to Gatwick an additional platform was constructed alongside No 4A. Numbered 4B, it was opened for public use on 5 May 1975. Although passenger traffic had ceased during 1965, the Southern yard continued to be used by goods traffic until February 1970, thereafter the few remaining sidings were used for storage purposes. The last siding in the yard was finally removed on 20 July 1975.

In August 1982 the remains of the Southern station were demolished (the garage had closed a few months earlier), and for a number of years the site continued to be used as additional car parking for the nearby Western Region station. However, the subsequent redevelopment of the area during the last three or four years has seen the complete site covered with a large office complex, the Apex Plaza, together with a new ticket hall/shopping arcade for the recently modernised ex-Great Western station.

Passenger Services

At approximately six o'clock on Monday 30 March 1840 the first passenger train left Reading for London, hauled by the locomotive *Fire Fly*. It is reported that during the day some 17 trains arrived and departed, all it seems well loaded. The first timetable gave an hourly service in each direction with the first down service from Paddington to Reading departing at 8.00am. Journey times ranged from 1hr 15min on the 'fasts' to 2hr 50min on the evening goods. The novelty of this new form of transport attracted vast numbers of passengers during these early days, so much so that the *Reading Mercury* reported that on Friday 17 April the seven o'clock service was so heavily loaded that two locomotives were required to pull it. It must be remembered that fares from Reading to London were not exactly cheap at 8s first, 5s 6d second and 3s third class. Trains at this time usually comprised three open seconds (216 passengers) and three firsts (96). It was not until the Great Western had reached Reading that 'persons of the lower station in life' (ordinary working folk) were carried at all. These poor wretches were carried on the evening mixed goods in open trucks which were usually placed next to the locomotive, as the following rules explain 'The goods train passengers will be conveyed in uncovered trucks by the goods train only, and 14lbs of luggage allowed for each'. This appalling contempt by the company for the lower classes resulted in many 'fatalities whilst in conveyance', and it was to take Gladstone's Railway Regulation Act of November 1844 to stop the practice. This Act compelled all railway companies (for the Great Western was not the only culprit) to provide seats and proper covered accommodation for their passengers, to run at least one stopping train daily in each direction at a speed of not less than 12mph including stops, and to charge only one penny a mile. These were known as 'cheap trains'. Passengers were obviously not yet used to the new form of transport, with many apparently arriving late at the station and thereby missing their trains. This resulted in the *Reading Mercury* printing the following advice:

'It is highly important that the public should bear in mind the absolute necessity of passengers procuring their tickets at least five minutes before the departure of each train.'

With the opening through to Bristol in June 1841, Reading became an important stopping place for the express services to and from Bristol, and for the branch trains to Hungerford from December 1847 and Basingstoke from November 1848. The timetable for 1842 shows seven through trains each way to Bristol and beyond, all calling at Reading. Intermediate services between Paddington and Reading comprised a 7.30am all stations up service with down services at 4.00pm and 7.30pm, this latter service calling at all stations to Swindon. Through services from Paddington to Exeter were introduced during May 1844. Services opened with eight down and seven up trains each taking on average some $7\frac{1}{2}$hr to reach their destination; all stopped at Reading. The first down train left Paddington at 6.00am reached Reading at 7.10am and eventually reached Exeter at 1.45pm. The first up train left Exeter at 7.00am. Third class passengers were conveyed in the 8.55pm down goods service, which reached Exeter at 4.05am. During 1845 the Great Western speeded up the Exeter services and although the Reading stop was retained, the running time to Exeter was reduced to just $4\frac{1}{2}$hr. On 12 June 1844 the Oxford Railway was opened, and this resulted in an extra morning stopping service which left Oxford at 7.50am calling at Reading at 9.00am. The evening 7.30pm down service now ran through to Oxford instead of Swindon. Mail continued to be handled using the ordinary mixed services. However, from 1 February 1855 a special 'Night Mail' was inaugurated between Paddington and Bristol. Leaving London at 8.46pm, it called at Reading just before 10.00pm. Of the early stopping services a particularly interesting train, inaugurated during October 1863, was the 12 o'clock through service via Kensington, to London Victoria.

It is also worth mentioning at this point early slip coach working at Reading. The first slip services to Reading were inaugurated during the summer of 1864, with coaches being slipped from some of the up Bristol services. The one-sided layout at the station required these to be diverted across the down tracks and into the up station, an interesting manoeuvre to say the least. From May 1869 the up 'Flying Dutchman', the Great Western's crack train at the time, also slipped a coach at Reading. The importance of slip coach working on the Great Western can be seen from the fact that by 1897 the number of slips at Reading had risen to 13, an all-time high, but by 1910 the number had dropped back to nine. Interestingly, one of these was a down service slipped from the 6.10pm express to South Wales. On arrival at Reading it was attached to an all stations stopping service to Oxford. As with many other services, slip coach working was more or less suspended for the duration of World War 1.

In October 1861 standard gauge services were inaugurated between the West Midlands and Paddington, with an initial service of three trains daily in each direction. In anticipation of this a pair of additional platforms were erected at Reading alongside the mixed lines, the station itself not being mixed until 1869. The first standard gauge train to arrive at Reading was the 9.35am service from Paddington to Birmingham. Hauled by 2-2-2 No 75, built by Beyer Peacock in April 1856, it reached Reading some 52min later at 10.27am. On 1 May 1863 a new service was inaugurated between Birkenhead, Dover and Hastings, with through carriages being conveyed on the 8.45am service to Paddington. Travelling via Birmingham and Oxford, the train reached Reading at 2.30pm. Here the through coaches were removed and conveyed to the South Eastern tracks via the Tunnel Junction. Running via Redhill, where a 20min luncheon break was taken, the train reached Dover at 6.50pm. The Hastings portion ran via Tonbridge and arrived at 6.30pm, and on the return working the lunch break was taken at Reading. The service did not last for long and was discontinued in October 1866.

Passenger services during the winter months seemed to suffer greatly from delays and cancellations due to both fog and snow. In January 1881 services in the Reading area and the Thames Valley as a whole were stopped for several days due to a particularly heavy snow storm. Reports state that the violent northeast winds carried the snow from the uplands and filled every ditch and railway cutting for many miles around Reading. Several trains apparently ran into these drifts and were completely buried, with it seems, in some cases, only the oil lamp covers in the carriage roofs and the melting snow from the heat of the locomotive to show where the train was engulfed. Several casualties were reported and it was several days before the line was clear.

The spread of the standard gauge was rapid and by the summer of 1877 of the 51 passenger trains leaving Paddington daily, only 12 were still broad gauge. Interestingly enough, one of these was a stopping train to Reading, but by the following year this also became a standard gauge service. By the end of the following decade the only broad gauge trains passing through Reading were the services to Bristol and the South-west, together with the odd goods. The end of the broad gauge was nigh, and on Friday 20 May 1892 at approximately 5.50pm the

last down broad gauge passenger service, the 5.00pm from Paddington to Plymouth, passed through Reading.

The continued growth of the population in the area, together with the increasing length of trains saw the need for a new station at Reading. The old one was hopelessly inadequate, and was subsequently rebuilt between 1896-99. The work to quadruple the tracks between Taplow and Didcot was started in 1890 and completed as far as Reading on 4 June 1893. This together with the new station now allowed the services, particularly secondary ones, to be expanded. Some new cross-country trains were also established at this time, in 1891 between Oxford and Basingstoke via Reading West curve and in the summer of 1897 a service of through coaches between Birkenhead and Folkestone. These were attached to the normal 8.15am Birkenhead-Paddington service, and slipped at Reading at 1.24pm. From here they were conveyed to Redhill, where they were then attached to the 2.45pm continental service from London to Folkestone. The opening of the new connection between the Great Western and the South Eastern Railway at Reading on 17 December 1899 saw these services use this connection instead of the skew tunnel. In 1903 a new service was introduced between Birkenhead and Deal. Leaving Birkenhead at 9.25am, Deal was reached at 6.30pm, while the up train left Deal at 11.00am and arrived at Birkenhead at 9.10pm. It was known to Reading men as the 'Continental'. The service was withdrawn in October 1916 because of the war. After a gap of some five years, it was reinstated on 10 July 1922 as a full restaurant car service to Dover and Margate.

Another particularly interesting service that was inaugurated during 1893, was the 5.45pm through train from Paddington to Southampton. This ran via Reading and Newbury, from where it took the DN&S route to Winchester and Southampton. In 1900 the Great Central branch from Woodford to Banbury was opened, and in 1902 a new luncheon corridor express was inaugurated to run between Newcastle and Bournemouth West via Banbury, Reading West Junction and Basingstoke. At this time no stop was made at Reading but in 1906 this situation was resolved by the opening on 1 July of Reading West. This new station was situated just to the south of Oxford Road Junction, and was opened specifically as an interchange station for the cross-country services. On 2 July of the same year the final section of the new cut-off route to Taunton, between Castle Cary and Cogland Junction, was opened to passenger traffic. The new shorter route allowed the West of England services to be accelerated, although for a number of years the majority of the trains to the South-west continued to run via Bristol.

Between 1888 and 1912 the Great Western had progressively speeded up its fast services. This can be seen from the following net average journey times of passenger trains between Paddington and Reading; in 1888 this was 46min, in 1900 it was 44min and in 1912 it was 42min. At the turn of the century there were ten 44min direct trains to Reading from London whilst in the up direction there were 14. Of these only seven were direct and each took 47min to reach the capital.

In 1906 the Great Western extended its line through to Fishguard and one of the new services on the route was the 8.45am 'Irish Mail' boat train which for many years included a stop at Reading for both the up and down trains.

Services continued to increase, and by 1910 some 83 up and 82 down trains daily were calling at or originating from Reading. Figures for 1912 show passenger and parcels receipts amounting to £128,406 and the number of passengers booked was 539,082.

The following table is taken from the station working notice of December 1909 and shows the number of passenger services using each platform over a 24hr period. The table shows trains actually stopping at Reading and does not include goods or non-stop services.

Down Services

Platform 1	29 trains + 1 slip
Platform 2	7 trains
Platform 3	6 trains
Platform 5	27 trains
Platform 1 West Bay	5 trains
Platform 3 West Bay	1 train
Platform 5 East Bay	3 trains
Platform 5 West Bay	3 trains
	Total 82

Up Services

Platform 4	24 trains + 7 slips
Platform 6	31 trains + 2 slips
Platform 4 East Bay	1 train
Platform 6 East Bay	4 trains
Platform 1 West Bay	14 trains
	Total 83

Suburban services on the Great Western gradually evolved over the years as more and more of the population of London spread into the Bucks and Berks countryside. During the early years these ran mainly between Paddington and Slough but by the turn of the century many of them had been extended as far as Reading. With Reading's adjacency to the Thames, the Great Western and the South Eastern ran many combined rail, road and river trips. Operated in conjunction with Salters Steamers of Oxford, these became very popular over the years and formed an important part of the railway and tourist trade at Reading well into Western Region days.

On 4 May 1914 steam railmotor services were inaugurated between Reading, Twyford and Henley, and also between Reading and Basingstoke. One railmotor initially worked three of the daily services to Henley departing at 10.56am, 2.20pm and 3.43pm.

A steam railmotor, possibly No 34, passes the small signalbox at Earley on its approach to Reading with an afternoon service from Henley. The green fields behind the railmotor became the site of the wartime-constructed, but now demolished, CEGB Earley power station. *B. Davis collection*

A second motor worked the 12.15pm and 5.55pm services to Basingstoke. The steam railmotors continued to operate in the Reading area until December 1934, when they were withdrawn and replaced by the new AEC diesel railcars.

Apart from the Sonning accident of Christmas Eve 1841, which is described in Chapter 1, accidents of any magnitude at Reading have been few and far between. One, however, that deserves a mention happened on the morning of 17 June 1914. A race special on its way to Ascot and hauled by 'Bulldog' class 4-4-0 No 3379 *Reading,* had stopped at the up platform to effect a crew change. It appears that someone, anxious to get the special away, gave the new crew the right of way without checking the platform starting signal. The crew obviously did not check the signal either, and promptly pulled away just as a fast service from Worcester, hauled by 'County' class 4-4-0 No 3819 *County of Leicester,* was passing through on the up main avoiding line.

By this time the 'Bulldog' had fouled the main line and the two engines struck a glancing blow, the 'County' together with several of the carriages was derailed. Luckily none of the passengers in either train was seriously hurt but unfortunately the driver of the Worcester train, Peter Young, was killed. As with many railway accidents, it had been caused solely by human error. The crash had also blocked the normal connection to the South Eastern lines at East Junction. This necessitated, possibly for the only time this century, the diversion of a passenger train, the through service from Birkenhead to Dover, via the goods-only Tunnel Junction line.

During World War 1 Reading became a major centre for military traffic moving between the North and the South. By the end of hostilities, Reading itself had dealt with some 136 hospital trains. Many special services were run over the years in connection with the races at Newbury. Apart from the race specials from Paddington, probably the

Above:
Ex-LSWR 'L11' 4-4-0 No 156 and an unidentified Churchward Mogul stand in the west bay platforms at Reading with Basingstoke and Newbury line services.
Lens of Sutton

Right:
The aftermath of the accident at Reading on 17 June 1914, showing the damage to the engine of the Race Special, Bulldog class No 3387 *Reading.*
G. A. Carpenter collection

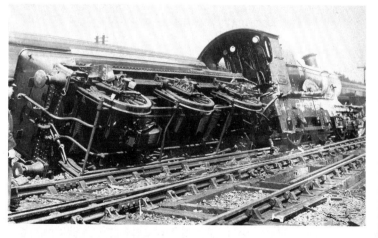

most popular were the extra services that were run on race days from Reading. Up until World War 2 these were sometimes loaded with up to 10 or 12 coaches, with standing room only! During the period between the wars and with many of the main line express services restored, Reading became as busy as ever. On 21 October 1924 the GWR introduced a new bus service between Reading station and Twyford, which ran via Woodley and Sonning village, and thus alleviated the need for the GW to construct a halt platform at Sonning. The service

Top:
This photograph taken in August 1923 shows Churchward's Pacific No 111 *The Great Bear,* standing at the down relief platform at Reading with the 10.45 service to Bristol and Cheltenham. Notice also the interesting signals. *V. R. Webster*

Above:
'6100' class 2-6-2T No 6145 stands in the down bay at Reading on 12 May 1951 with a service to Newbury, from where the ex-Great Western diesel railcar in the adjacent bay has just arrived. *P. J. Kelley*

was operated over the years using examples of both Chevrolet and Maudslay buses; it was discontinued during 1933.

During 1927 the first of the newly constructed 'King' class engines started to appear on the services to the South-west. In the 1930s the Thames Valley suburban services were once again improved and accelerated. This was accomplished with the introduction of new rolling stock together with the new Collett '6100' class 2-6-2T locomotives. The service now gave some 25 local trains each way daily between Reading and Paddington, and another 22 westwards to Didcot and Oxford. There were also four daily through services to Henley and no fewer than 17 to Basingstoke, a total that included three through services to Portsmouth and four to Southampton. For the summer months through coaches from Reading were available to such places

as Aberystwyth, Barmouth, Stokes Bay, Weymouth, Minehead, Southampton Docks, Torquay and Weston-super-Mare.

As already mentioned, the 1930s also saw the arrival of the new AEC diesel railcars. The first of these officially entered service on 5 February 1934 after running for several weeks on trials, and although officially allocated to Southall, it operated four services daily between Reading and Didcot and two daily between Reading and Henley. By 1938 two railcars were operating from Reading, covering a number of the services to Henley, Didcot and Newbury.

The great holiday boom of the 1930s saw Reading become a very busy station indeed. The bulk of the holiday traffic to the Devon and Cornish resorts ran

Left:
The ex-Great Western diesel railcars formed an important part of the local passenger workings in the Reading area for nearly 30 years. Here cars Nos 33 and 38 arrive at Reading with the 7.45am service from Slough to Newbury. *R. A. Panting*

Below left:
Collett 0-4-2T No 1407 departs from platform 9 at Reading with an afternoon service to Twyford and Henley. *B. Davis collection*

Below:
Adams 'A12' class 'Jubilee' No 617 stands at platform 3 at Reading on 5 June 1930, having arrived with an all stations service from Southampton. *OURS collection*

via the Berks & Hants route, and working timetables for summer Saturdays during this time show trains for Exeter and beyond passing through Reading every 40min. Slip coach working was once again at its peak during this time with no fewer than nine up slips each weekday. Passenger journeys from Reading at this time had risen to almost 800,000 annually. During this time there were many through services from the North to the South using the junctions at either end of Reading. To the east, restaurant car services from Birkenhead and Birmingham travelled via the 1899 junction to reach the resorts of Ramsgate, Margate and Hastings, whilst through services from Sheffield, Newcastle, York and Bradford to Portsmouth, Bournemouth and Poole used the West Junction. Although this latter group of trains avoided Reading General, many called at Reading West. A feature of the timetable during the 1930s was the inclusion of a through carriage between Portsmouth and Manchester, which was added to the Bournemouth to Birkenhead service at Eastleigh.

Unfortunately just as in the 1914-18 conflict, World War 2 also brought to an end many of these cross-country workings. One such service which had continued to run during the war was a buffet car train from Newcastle to Ashford. Although essentially designated a troop leave train, a limited number of tickets were made available for public use, and such was the popularity of this service it appears that it was regularly loaded with up to 17 carriages. Wartime traffic, however, still made Reading a busy junction and this was clearly

Above left:
Summer holiday time as 'King Arthur' No 30740 *Merlin* winds its way into Reading West with a service from Sheffield and Bradford to Bournemouth in July 1955. *C. R. L. Coles*

Left:
Tilehurst station falls within the Reading town boundary, and was opened during 1882. Here on 17 September 1955, 'King Arthur' No 30736 *Excalibur* hurries through with a service from the Midlands to Bournemouth. *R. C. Riley*

Below left:
The through service from Dover to Birkenhead hauled by 'U' class No 1611 enters Reading via the 1899 incline connection on 5 August 1939. *V. R. Webster*

Above:
'Britannia' Pacific No 70024 *Vulcan* enters Reading on 1 April 1959, with the 1.55pm service from Paddington to Pembroke Dock. *Ian Allan Library*

illustrated firstly on 1 September 1939 when some 25,000 Londoners, both adults and children, were evacuated to Reading and again during the evacuation of Dunkirk when between 27 May and 4 June 1940 normal services over the Reading-Redhill line were suspended. Between these dates some 565 troop trains left the Channel ports, with 293 of them running through to both the Great Western and Southern stations at Reading.

On 25 May 1941 East Spur Junction was opened. It saw immediate use with many troop and military supply trains, but equally importantly it allowed heavy coal trains from South Wales to reach Battersea power station without passing through central London. The new connection came into its own passenger-wise after the war, when the cross country services were gradually resorted to pre-war levels. The holiday boom of the 1950s saw many new cross country services introduced. During the summer of 1958, for example, the service of through inter regional trains on Saturdays using the junctions at Reading comprised 10 via the 'New Junction' and Redhill line and 28 via the West Junction and Basingstoke (totals include both up and down services). On 2 April 1950 the Basingstoke branch became part of the Southern Region, with local services to and from Reading being operated with Southern stock and crews. The local service over the branch comprised 12 trains a day in each direction, with through services to both Portsmouth and Southampton. Apart from the many local, semi-fast and cross-country trains, we must also remember that Reading was also passed by a number of express services, many of which had slipped a coach here before the war. Sadly after the war slip coach working did not revert to the pre-war levels and by 1955 services to Reading had dropped to just three up slips daily, from the 8.30am Plymouth (the 'Mayflower' from 1957), the 4.05pm Weymouth and the 1.50pm Bristol. The end of the summer services in 1958 also brought to an end slip coach working at Reading, the last slip being made at approximately 3.25pm on 12 September from the 1.50pm up Bristol. The first two had been discontinued several months earlier, and the new winter timetable now showed all three of these services making a call at Reading. In 1959 suburban services started to pass from steam to diesel traction when diesel multiple-units were introduced on Paddington-Oxford local services from the start of the winter timetable.

Another milestone was passed when in 1962 the ex-GW diesel railcars were withdrawn from passenger services in the Reading area, after being a feature of the local services for some 28 years. During the 1950s the three cars based at Reading were clocking up some 650 miles a day, covering duties between Newbury and Lambourn, Henley and Maidenhead, and Reading and Newbury.

Top:
This fine view of the east end of Reading shows Hymek No D7031 leaving on the 4.45pm service from Weston-super-Mare to Paddington. The entrance to the low level yard is on the right. Also in view is the small high level ground frame hut and the large Goods Lines East signalbox. *B. Davis collection*

Above:
Carrying green livery with yellow warning panels, 'Warship' class No D851 *Temeraire* approaches Reading with the 11.35am service from Weston-super-Mare to Paddington on 17 October 1964. *G. T. Robinson*

During 1958 some of the main line services to Bristol and Plymouth passed from steam to diesel-hydraulic traction. This new form of motive power now allowed stops to be made at Reading without the time penalty that occurred with steam traction, and by the end of 1964 the only Class 1 passenger services on the Western Region still rostered for steam haulage were the three cross-country services from Bournemouth to Oxford and beyond, plus a couple in the Birmingham area. All other main line services passing through Reading were diesel powered. The acceleration of services can be seen from the allowed point to point times taken from the 1962 and 1964 working timetables for non-stop Paddington-Reading trains loaded to 350 tons. In 1962 the allowance for a 'Castle' class locomotive was 38min, whereas in 1964 the allowance for Class 47 and 52 diesels was only 30½min. Today the Class 47s and 50s on the Network Express services have a scheduled booked time of 34min.

From 5 September 1964 the through services between the Midlands and the Kent coast were withdrawn. These had been a feature of the timetable at Reading since 1899, although from

11 September 1961 this service, which had previously started from Birkenhead, was cut back to Wolverhampton. During 1962 the local service to Basingstoke was dieselised using the newly built three-car 'Hampshire' sets. From the start of the 1966 winter timetable, steam traction was withdrawn from the cross-country services between Oxford and Bournemouth. The subsequent switch to diesel traction now saw Reading West all but abandoned in favour of a reversal at Reading General. A general cut-back of cross-country services over the Bournemouth line during 1967 saw the

Top:
Class 52 'Western' diesel-hydraulic No D1011 *Western Thunderer* **leaves Reading with a service from Penzance, as fellow 'Western' No D1009** *Western Invader,* **waits on the up fast line with a Yeoman stone train, on 2 August 1973.** *S. Creer*

Above:
Berkshire Class 205 unit No 1129 is seen here approaching Reading with the 11.24 service from Salisbury on 7 April 1976, whilst a pair of Class 33 diesels, Nos 33024 and 33114, wait to leave the diesel depot. *Brian Morrison*

Above:
Hawksworth 'County' class No 1002 *County of Berks* passes under the A4 roadbridge at Sonning Cutting with the 11.15am service from Paddington to Worcester on 2 March 1963. *M. Pope*

Below:
This view from Western Tower shows the 10.29 Poole-Birmingham New Street arriving at Reading in the mid-1960s behind a Brush Type 4 locomotive. *C. T. Gifford*

'Pines Express' withdrawn from the timetable from 4 June. This one time Somerset & Dorset service had been switched to the Reading route in September 1962. It was to take five years before the services were expanded once again, and for the 1972 Summer timetable the existing services were supplemented with through services from Weymouth, Poole and Bournemouth to Leeds, Manchester and Liverpool. An added feature of the new timetable was the addition, for the first time, of a Sunday service.

On Monday 6 March 1967 Motorail services were switched from Slough to Reading. The new terminal loading bay was situated at the west end of the station, on the site of the old cattle pens. Two services were provided from Reading, the 10.10 Thursday, Friday and Saturdays-only service to Fishguard and the 8.40 Monday, Wednesday and Saturdays only service to St Austell. The continuing growth of passenger traffic locally, together with the cramped conditions of the station booking hall, saw the opening during November 1970 of a new travel centre in the shopping arcade alongside the Western Tower. Gradually during the 1970s the hydraulics were withdrawn and were initially replaced by Class 47 and 50 motive power. However, in 1976 the

Western Region was hit by the high speed revolution as gradually, from 4 October, the new HSTs were introduced on to the Bristol and South Wales services. Many of these, of course, stopped at Reading and soon offered timings to Paddington (27min), Bristol (57min) and Cardiff (88min) which would be difficult to beat even with electrification. The summer timetable of 1979 also saw the introduction of HSTs on to the South-west route. Four sets operated eight services a day between Paddington, Exeter and Plymouth. During August of the same year the last locomotive-hauled 'Cornish Riviera' ran, and by 1980 almost all of the main South-west services were in the hands of the HSTs. Timings were accelerated, with the journey time from Reading to Exeter being reduced from an average of 2hr 40min to just 1hr 55min.

The timetable of 14 May 1979 saw the introduction of a new daily two-train through service between Manchester and Brighton, via Oxford, Kensington Olympia and East Croydon. Although there were no longer any cross-country trains using the old South Eastern route out of Reading, services over this line were improved with the introduction on 12 May 1980 of a new hourly interval service between Reading and Gatwick. An innovation for the start of the summer timetable on 17 May 1982 was the introduction of a new through service between Paddington and Glasgow. This did not last for long, as from 14 May 1984 the service was diverted to run to and from Poole and was named the 'Wessex Scot'. This chapter can only but summarise the growth of the services over the years and more recent developments are covered in Chapter 11, Reading Today.

Left:
The 1.45pm service from Paddington to Weston-super-Mare stands at Reading on 27 December 1967, double-headed by 'Warship' No D859 *Vanquisher* and the unique No D0280 *Falcon*. *D. E. Canning*

Below left:
Successors to the Class 52 'Westerns' on West of England services were the 50 members of Class 50. No 50046 *Ajax* passes the brick shell of Main Line West box as it arrives at platform 5 with the 07.50 service from Paignton to Paddington on 14 July 1979. *M. Yarwood*

Below:
Class 33 No 33001 awaits departure from Reading with the 07.02 Newcastle-Poole on Saturday 1 February 1975. In the background is Class 47 No 47081 *Odin* on station pilot duty and a Class 117 DMU on the 13.15 to Oxford. *G. Roy Hounsell*

Goods Services

Reading has always been an important centre for goods operations and for a town of its size it was provided over the years with some excellent facilities. From the turn of the century Reading became the headquarters of a goods district that encompassed within its area Didcot, Oxford, Winchester, Devizes, Staines and Uxbridge. As already mentioned in Chapter 1, the coming of the railway saw the town grow commercially, with most of this new industry using the railway. The Great Western was obviously aware of this potential from the start, as early plans show that both the up and down platforms at the old station were each provided with their own separate goods shed. These were apparently of an open design and the roofs which contained skylights were supported on a series of pillars. Within the sheds were situated the offices of the District Engineer, the Goods Manager and the Telegraph Superintendent. The space between the two goods sheds was occupied by a cattle and horse loading bank, two carriage docks with a traversing table, and two wagon turntables for working traffic in and out of the sheds. In 1863 the goods department was expanded when the pair of wagon turntables together with the traverser were removed. The two old sheds were then linked by the addition of a new goods shed, which was built in the resulting gap. Also about this time the Great Western constructed a transfer shed at Reading: details of this shed have proved difficult to find, but it appears to have been situated to the east of the station.

Great Western goods services at this time consisted mainly of mixed goods, livestock and coal trains. A feature of the timetable for many years was an evening horse train to the capital, and this also carried third class passengers! These services remained strictly broad gauge for many years but from 1856 standard gauge goods trains, consisting mostly of coal and perishable traffic, ran between Wolverhampton and Basingstoke via Reading West Junction over the newly mixed track. Standard gauge goods services were inaugurated between the Midlands and London during 1861. By 1879 goods services at Reading had expanded to some 50 trains a day in each direction. These comprised general goods, minerals, milk, fish and horsebox trains.

In 1880 the locomotive department moved to a new site, thus allowing the goods department to take

48

over and use the now vacated broad gauge locomotive shed. This continued to be used until the station rebuilding work of 1896 saw the shed closed and the site cleared. In order to replace this, a brand new goods depot had been opened on 15 June of the same year. It was built on a lower level to the main line, on a stretch of land that was adjacent to both Vastern Road and Kings Meadow. Incidentally, it was here that the Reading Races were once held. Part of this depot comprised an extensive coal and mileage yard. This section was situated to the west of the depot buildings and containing some 26 sidings, which were capable of holding nearly 700 wagons. Within this yard was also situated a 20 ton

URGENT.
HUNTLEY & PALMERS
BISCUITS
SHUNT WITH GREAT CARE

Above left:
The goods staff at Kings Meadow, photographed around the turn of the century. *Great Western Trust*

Left:
Fashions change somewhat, as can be seen in this picture of the goods staff, again at Kings Meadow, in 1945. *D. Embury*

Above:
Huntley & Palmers label. *D. Castle collection*

weighbridge together with cattle and horse docks. To the east, and lying alongside the Kings Meadow Road was the main 'Low Level' goods depot. Known locally as the new shed, the double sided building was constructed of brick. The main structure measured approximately 300ft × 50ft and was capable of holding some 40 wagons. It contained two loading platforms each fitted with hydraulic cranes capable of lifting up to 10 tons. Situated above on a second floor was a large grain warehouse giving a total storage area of some 1,100sq yd. Office accommodation for the 39 goods clerks engaged here was provided at the western end of the main building. Hydraulic power for the various cranes,

lifts and capstans was supplied from the hydraulic house. This was situated alongside the high level entrance to the yard and contained a stationary boiler which together with various pumps supplied some 20,000gal of water a day. The sidings adjacent to the goods shed were capable of holding about 240 wagons, and were connected to the mileage yard by way of the Vastern Road level crossing. In later years because of the increase in road traffic this was only used at night. A low-level connection was also provided between this yard to both the Huntley & Palmers factory and the Gas Works. Huntley & Palmers was certainly the biggest customer locally: figures for 1935 show that some 15,000 wagons and 52,000 tons of goods were passing in and out of the biscuit factory sidings annually. Adjacent to the goods shed was a 30 ton capacity cart weighbridge. Coal formed an important commodity at Reading with much traffic arriving locally for the gas works, the two locomotive depots and also the town trade. Much of the coal traffic for the gas works was delivered via the South Eastern yard.

Most of the goods traffic at Reading was generally dealt with at the West Junction Marshalling Sidings. From here traffic was re-sorted and sent out to the various stations, branches and military establishments in the area. The West sidings had been extensively remodelled and enlarged around the

Above:
Ex-Great Western 2-8-0 No 3854 leaves the yards at Reading and crosses on to the down relief line at Scours Lane with a mixed goods for Didcot and Oxford circa 1959. *C. J. Blay*

Right:
'Dukedog' 4-4-0 No 9028 of Croes Newydd shed approaches Scours Lane Junction from the west, with a horsebox special. *C. J. Blay*

turn of the century. New up and down yards were added on the north side of the main line, each containing 10 sidings. Together with the old up and down yards that were still in use, this gave a total of 58 sidings. These provided accommodation for something approaching 1,500 wagons, although over the years part of the old up yard was given over to use for wagon repairs. Both the Bridge and Permanent Way engineering departments were also situated here, the latter being responsible for an area which extended from Kennington Junction to Southall, and also included Princes Risborough, Northolt Junction, Newbury, Winchester and Basingstoke. Over the years the railway at Reading seems to have been plagued with fires, and yet another occurred at the Permanent Way depot workshops on the evening of Monday 31 July 1905. The depot was luckily situated close to the Caversham Road fire station, and quick attention by the brigade kept damage to a minimum.

Slightly further west were the exchange sidings and yard at Scours Lane, Tilehurst. This yard contained three through lines and a further 10 sidings, one of which served a nearby cold store. The yard was constructed during World War 1, and saw a considerable interchange of traffic over the years — particularly from the Southern lines, with services arriving daily from Dover, Redhill, Ashford, Angerstein Wharf (Charlton) and Feltham. Prior to World War 1 these services had run into the West

Junction Yards. A twice daily local trip working also provided an interchange of traffic between Scours Lane and the low level southern yard. Each of the goods yards at Reading was supplied with shunting engines. West Junction Yard was the busiest and was provided with no less than four, with the up yard here being shunted 24hr a day.

The Great Western always treated its goods customers with great importance. It soon became apparent that for many of the traders at Reading, the existing goods facilities, excellent though they were, were all rather inconveniently situated on the northern outskirts of the town. This caused many problems with large loads having to traverse the narrow streets and tram routes of the town centre. In order to alleviate the problem, the Great Western constructed a new 'central' goods depot to the south of the town. The site chosen was adjacent to both the Kennet & Avon Canal and the Holy Brook. In fact the land had previously been used by the canal company for warehousing and wharfage purposes. Rather interestingly, prior to construction starting, the Great Western was also required to resite a Masonic Temple which also stood on the site.

Situated mainly in the Coley area of the town, the 1¾ mile connecting line from Southcote Junction on the Berks & Hants became known as the Coley branch. It must be said that this was no ordinary branch line, as the only type of Great Western locomotive that was restricted from using it was a 'King'! The new depot was constructed by Messrs H. Lovatt & Co of Wolverhampton and was opened on 4 May 1908, with entrance to the yard being effected from nearby Fobney Street. All types of traffic were handled here, including coal, timber, bricks, stone and grain, together with much incoming and outgoing traffic for the nearby Simonds Brewery. An exchange of goods traffic between the railway and the nearby Kennet was made via a siding to the adjacent Bear Wharf. The yard which had its own goods shed and offices was also fitted with a 10-ton lifting crane and 20-ton cart weighbridge, which together with various other lifting cranes, both fixed and mobile, made the loading and unloading of wagons an easy task. The yard contained 12 lines of sidings, which were capable of holding some 300 wagons. For ease of loading and unloading these sidings were divided into pairs, each being provided

Above left:
The neat and tidy layout at Reading Central goods depot circa 1919. *L&GRP*

Left:
Collett 0-6-0 No 2245 stands at the Central goods depot, terminus of the Coley branch on 3 November 1956. *Hugh Davis*

Above:
Women railway employees working at the Central goods depot on 20 April 1943. *B. Davis collection*

with its own roadway. Various additional sidings also served Simonds Brewery, Esso Petroleum and the Co-operative preserve works. The yard was put to good use when it was employed as the railhead for the unloading of livestock and machinery for the Royal County Show. This was held at the nearby Prospect Park on 10 June 1909, and it was reported that the show had some 40,000 visitors.

In later years Central Goods was fed by a twice daily trip from West Junction. For some reason the GWR never installed locomotive watering facilities here, so a tank type shunting locomotive was not normally provided due to its limited water capacity, and instead the train locomotive, which was usually a tender type, would be used to shunt the yard. All in all it was an excellent facility and used in conjunction with the other yards gave Reading a goods service that was second to none for a town of its size.

Between 5 and 10 July 1926, the 85th Royal Agricultural Show was held at Reading and in order to deal with the vast amount of both livestock and machinery arriving here, the Great Western constructed a temporary loading platform in the low level goods yard at Kings Meadow. The platform which measured some 725ft long and 42ft wide was reached by a specially constructed roadway. Alongside this, a temporary stable block was constructed in order to accommodate the vast numbers of horses arriving. A report in the *GW Magazine* of the time states that apart from the arrival of all of the machinery there were 22 special livestock trains and some 138 horse boxes dealt with in the week prior to the start of the show. In 1929 the GWR introduced nicknames for some of their more important goods services, with the 10.30pm service from Reading to Laira becoming known as 'The Biscuit'. Not to be outdone, it seems that Southern drivers at Reading also used the same nickname for the 7.15pm fast service from Reading South to Feltham. During World War 2, Reading became an important interchange point for cross-country goods and military traffic. In order to speed the flow of this traffic a new junction was opened between the GW and SE lines to the east of Reading on 16 March 1941. Throughout the period of the war the new junction saw very heavy military use, as indeed did the Basingstoke branch with both ammunition and stores trains running to and from the MOD depot at Bramley. As with many other places Reading suffered from congestion at this time and to help alleviate the problem extra goods loops and refuge sidings were constructed in the area. Together with the existing sidings this gave the following wagon capacities: in the *down direction* Reading Spur 60, Reading 464, Reading West Junction 50 and Tilehurst 44, and in the *up direction*, Tilehurst 43, Scours Lane 457, Reading East to Reading Spur 61 and Sonning 56. After the war the goods services in the area reverted back to prewar levels, with approximately 150 freight services daily using the yards in the area. Many of these services to such places as Bordesley, Birkenhead, Tavistock Junction, Banbury, Bristol and Cardiff had been a feature of the timetable from well before the turn of the century. In 1958 proposals were made to form a new outer orbital goods route around London, and part of the work would have seen the reinstatement and improvement of the Tunnel Junction at Reading.

Although some of the work, such as the flyover at Bletchley was completed, the idea was never fully exploited and eventually it was abandoned.

With the rundown of the railways generally during the 1960s, together with the closure of many branch lines and small yards, and the switch of goods from rail to road, many of the yards locally became redundant. Scours Lane and the old West down yard were the first locally to succumb, being closed during 1968. The two low level yards were severed when on 7 August 1965 the Vastern Road level crossing was lifted. In December 1969 the Kings Meadow goods department was closed, and at the same time the rail connection into the Huntley & Palmers factory was removed. The large goods shed at Kings Meadow continued to be used for a time by

Below:
Southern 'Q1' class No 33026 leaves Scours Lane sidings on 10 October 1964 with the 3.25pm freight from Moreton to Redhill. *G. T. Robinson*

Right:
Urie 'S15' Class No 30501 approaches Reading General on 22 July 1955 with the 8.44am Feltham-Scours Lane mixed goods. The train has just left the Southern lines via 'New Spur Junction'. The old incline junction can be seen in the foreground. *M. Earley*

Below right:
Ex-Great Western '5700' class 0-6-0PT No 4661 passes through Reading with a down goods on 26 April 1958. *M. Yarwood*

National Carriers, but it was demolished in 1987 to make way for a new industrial park. The few remaining sidings in the Vastern Road yard together with the incline connection were removed during the same year, in preparation for the construction of the new car park. On the Coley branch, Bear wharf goods shed and sidings were closed from 20 March 1969, but the remaining sidings at Central Goods continued to be used until Monday 25 July 1983, when the yard was officially closed. The remaining track work on the Coley branch was finally lifted during January 1985.

Below:
An up van train hauled by Class 31 No 31256 passes the old Goods Lines West signalbox at Reading on 7 April 1976. *Brian Morrison*

Bottom:
Class 31 No 5695 stands on the Vastern Road bridge on 20 February 1974 with an emergency ballast train. Work on the bridge had caused the ballast to cave in at this point. This resulted in all electric services from Waterloo being terminated at Wokingham, and a DMU shuttle service running from there into platform 10 at Reading. *R. E. Ruffell*

The Great Western Station

The station at Reading today is of a very different design from that which was provided by Brunel for the opening of the line to Reading in 1840. This original station was a one-sided affair which was positioned on the town (south) side of the new railway. Constructed mainly of wood, its unusual design contained two separate platforms, lying end-to-end on the same section of track. Situated between the two platforms were a pair of goods sheds. These were served by a pair of wagon turntables. The resulting layout meant that Reading was effectively provided with what were essentially two separate stations, one for the up trains and the other for the down and each with its own loop. It was a design that Brunel had also used elsewhere, notably at Slough, where, as at Reading the town also lay to the south of the railway. The advantages with this type of design were that passengers did not have to cross the lines, and that non-stop trains ran clear of the station.

The buildings, which were enclosed on one side only, were constructed of framed timber and weather-board. Each platform was covered by its own overall roof, approximately 200ft in length, supported by a series of iron columns. Apparently because of the nature of the newly made-up land, the whole complex was stabilised using hundreds of wooden piles. The up station was also provided with a bay at the east end and a small island platform, access to which was via a wooden footbridge. It seems that this platform was used by up trains from the Hungerford and Basingstoke branches. Unusually this same facility was not provided on the down side, with trains from the branches using a bay platform here. It seems likely that both the up island platform and down bay were later additions to the original station. They were probably constructed during the autumn of 1847 in preparation for the Basingstoke and Hungerford services, as neither appear to be in evidence on a plan dated 31 July 1847. Each station was provided with its own individual entrance and booking hall. These impressive looking buildings were constructed in brick with slate roofs.

Services not stopping at Reading were able to pass the station via up and down avoiding lines. The underlying problem with this type of one-sided

Below:
This fine shot shows the many horse cabs waiting for custom outside the GW and SE stations. As with many other Great Western stations, a cab inspector was employed here to control the cabbies, many of whom were regularly fined or suspended from operating both for drunkenness and for the use of foul and abusive language. The large statue of King Edward VII, was presented to the town by Martin Sutton, founder of Suttons Seeds. *Author's collection*

G.W.R. STATION READING NO. 46

design meant that an up stopping train had to cross the down main line twice and also the down platform loop on entering the up station, so that only one train in either direction could be admitted at one time, and no down train could pass whilst an up train was coming in. These problems were obviously troubling Brunel for during 1853 he had himself sketched out two separate proposals for a new layout at Reading, but neither scheme was adopted.

The down station underwent some unscheduled alterations on the evening of 12 October 1853 when a broad gauge goods en route from Basingstoke to London was running through the station to shunt back on to the up main line. Unfortunately one of the old type bonnet iron trucks had its side flap half-down and held in position by a chain, tailboard fashion. This caught the row of cast iron columns and either cut them in two or knocked them over, causing the roof to collapse. The roof was subsequently replaced by a 'temporary' structure of a quite different design, which incredibly, was good enough to survive for another 40 years.

It soon became obvious that the old station was becoming inadequate for the amount of traffic now arriving at and departing from Reading. Since its construction in 1840 constant improvements had been made, but without altering the one sided layout. The opening of the Hungerford and Basingstoke branches in 1847 and 1848 respectively saw various alterations made to the trackwork at the west end of the station, and during this latter year the Caversham Road bridge was widened.

On 1 October 1861 standard gauge services were inaugurated between Paddington and Birmingham over the newly mixed gauge track. In order to utilise these new services without going to the expense of laying mixed trackwork into the already complicated layout of the old station, two new wooden platforms were erected on either side of the newly mixed lines and alongside the existing station. During September of the same year various alterations were made to the platform layout at Reading, the most notable alteration being the linking of the up and down platforms. The roof of the new section had a very temporary look about it, being covered it seems with nothing more than tarred felt. The construction of the linking platform had required the removal of the wagon turntables. It also appears that the pair of goods sheds were rebuilt to form a single shed. During 1863 the goods department was expanded, with the construction of a new transfer shed. This measured approximately 200ft×80ft, and was situated adjacent to the mixed gauge lines, at the east of the station. On 1 April 1869 the mixed gauge tracks were extended into the station proper, thus allowing the temporary mixed gauge platforms to be removed. Although many 'improvements' had been made to the station since its construction, it was still a rather sub-standard structure for an expanding town like Reading.

The Great Western was nothing if not sensitive to criticism for it appears that after many complaints from the local corporation regarding the rundown state of the station, a start had been made during the autumn of 1865 to rebuild at least the main entrance block. The new building was constructed in front of the old up station. It was built in yellow stock brick and Bath stone in the classic style, and a large central clock tower gave a degree of grandeur to the new entrance. It was completed and opened on Saturday 30 May 1868, and the old up station entrance block was then demolished, leaving it

seems quite a gap between the new building and the up platform. It must be mentioned however that the old down station entrance building and booking office was retained and continued to be used right up until the rebuilding work of 1896.

Although the new facade was a great improvement for the passengers, it was certainly not for the operating department, as the single-sided working arrangements were still in use. In 1880 the locomotive depot was moved to the west of the station and during the same year the goods depot was moved into the empty shed building. The old transfer shed subsequently fell out of use and was demolished within the year. There is no mention in the records as to the numbers of staff employed during the early years, but a station report of 1871 states that there were 114 employees at the Reading station, of which 21 were signalmen. It seems that at this time the station may have been known as Reading Central, but as yet it has not been possible to confirm this. Tickets issued around the 1890s simply show it as Reading. The removal of the broad gauge in 1892 also allowed a second track to be laid alongside the island platform, thus giving the station an extra platform for up trains, although two-way working was still in regular use on the combined up and down platforms.

With the constant increase in traffic over the ensuing years, Reading was rapidly becoming one

of, if not the busiest station on the Great Western system. What was still basically a one-sided layout was proving to be quite inadequate, and it was to be no real surprise when on 25 July 1896 work was started on the reconstruction of the old down station. Over a year before this, on 2 May 1895, a proposal had been made during a meeting of the town council that the new station should be a joint station used by all three operating companies. This idea was promptly turned down by the Great Western 'because of the problems of the different levels between the existing railways'.

In order to undertake the rebuilding work, the goods shed which had once served as a broad gauge engine shed at the opening of the line was demolished to allow room for the complete removal of the old layout and the construction of several new platforms. In order to allow for the reconstruction both the Caversham and Vastern Road bridges were rebuilt. The work on rebuilding the station was undertaken by Pattisons of Westminster at a cost of about £6,000. The reconstruction eventually took some three years to complete. The up relief platform was the first item to be finished, opening on 2 May 1898, and on 23 January 1899 the new booking office under the clock tower was complete and ready for use. It is worth reflecting that the company had now provided 10 platforms to accommodate the same number of services that once ran into the old station and this alone must clearly illustrate the operating problems of the old layout. On 5 February 1899 a new horse and carriage siding together with a new middle line siding were opened at the eastern end of the down main platform. One interesting proposal made at this time, but never followed through, was to link the new station to the nearby South Eastern

station with a covered walkway. The rebuilding work was not without its problems, as the then stationmaster, one Frederick Fraser, in a report to the company during the alterations, mentions the many complaints by passengers of both delays to services and the noise and dirt from the reconstruction work (it seems that nothing has changed!). The new layout now provided four main platforms and six bays, each covered by its own individual awning. This was the policy of the then chief engineer James Inglis, who did not favour providing overall roofs on intermediate stations. The fact that Reading was not provided with an overall roof produced much local criticism, with the new verandah type roofs being described in the local press as 'nothing more than tin umbrellas'.

The down main platform (No 1) measured 960ft long and 60ft wide; it was divided at the western end into three 400ft long bays, primarily for use by Basingstoke and Berks & Hants branch services and numbered 1 West Bay and platforms 2 and 3 respectively. Situated on platform 1 were the main dining and refreshment rooms, as well as offices for

Below:
This overall view shows the rebuilt Great Western station circa 1910. *Author's collection*

Right:
The large water tank and hydraulic house. At one time this was used to supply hydraulic power for the lifts at the nearby station. Electric power saw it fall out of use, and in this 1960s view it is in use as a Mechanical & Electrical Dept track maintenance workshop. *C. J. Blay*

the Stationmaster, Station Inspector and District Goods Manager, the cloak and waiting rooms and the main station bookstall. The new centre island platform measured 1,150ft in length and was 50ft wide, and its two main faces were numbered 4 and 5. Single bay platforms numbered 4 East Bay and 5 West Bay were provided at either end for Paddington and Oxford branch stopping trains. It was also provided with refreshment facilities and the usual waiting and cloak rooms. A second island platform (No 6) 900ft in length, served the up relief line, with a bay (No 6 East) for local trains at the London end. A down relief line was also provided between the up and down relief platforms. The up relief platform also contained the Assistant Stationmaster's office, luggage, waiting and cloak rooms but unusually no refreshment facilities. These various offices formed a barrier between the up and down goods avoiding lines that pass along the back of the platform. All of these buildings were constructed using red bricks with the doors and windows being framed with blue bricks.

An unusual feature of the new layout was the non-provision of a down main platform loop. Only an up fast loop was provided through the station and this was not apparently used for this purpose until about 1908. Prior to this it was used as an empty carriage siding, and up fasts used the platform line which was restricted to just 40mph. Passenger access to the new layout was via a 240ft long subway that ran through to the Caversham Road side, where a small booking office was situated. Hydraulic lifts for both passenger and goods use were provided for each platform. Hydraulic power for these was supplied from the large water tower and pump house that was situated on the north side of the line adjacent to the Vastern Road bridge. In later years the subway was divided along the centre to provide a second service subway for railway use only. This was and still is used for moving parcels and mail traffic between the platform lifts. Provisions for the loading and unloading of both horses and carriages were situated at the west end of the up relief and east end of the down main platforms. The whole station layout was controlled by two new signalboxes at Reading East and West. These were direct replacements for the older boxes of the same name. A third box, Reading Middle, was removed during the rebuilding work and was not initially replaced. The new box at Main Line West contained 185 levers and was the largest lever frame box on the Great Western, and being situated near the signal works it certainly seems that it was built as a showpiece box, probably to complement the new station. The East box (115 levers) was built in a similar style and was a direct replacement of an older East box which had been situated on the west side of the Vastern Road bridge prior to the station rebuilding of 1896.

By 1907 the station staff numbers had risen to 273. Within this figure is included nine temporary, seasonal staff. The reconstruction of the station, as already mentioned, necessitated the removal of the old goods depot. This however was more than compensated for by the construction of a new, much larger low level goods depot on the north side of the line and to the east of the station.

A feature on many Great Western stations at this time was the use of a station dog for charity collecting and Reading was no exception. These dogs were apparently trained to sit on their hind legs and beg to the passing travellers. Available records show that in March 1894 the dog at Reading was a collie named Jack. He died during February 1896 having collected some £98 for the widows and orphans fund. He was replaced on 11 March 1896 by another collie who was also named Jack. Records do not show how long this dog lasted, but by October 1908 the dog at Reading was a black retriever called Prince. He had been presented to the railway by Sir Rufus Isaacs during the same year and during his four years on the station collected some £220 11s 2¾d, again for the Great Western Widows and Orphans fund, made up it seems of 44,282 coins. Prince died on 28 October 1912 from ptomaine poisoning (a form of blood poisoning). During the same month he was replaced by another collie, who was also christened 'Prince' by his keeper Ticket Inspector Wood. I can find no record of a successor to the second Prince, so he could well have been the last station dog at Reading.

In 1931 the subway was subject to an experiment

Above:
Prince, pictured at Reading in the early 1920s. These collecting dogs were allowed to roam freely around the station: notice the collecting box on its back. Also in the picture is the Middle signalbox. *B. Davis collection*

Right:
For many generations Reading has proved to be a mecca for trainspotters. This picture, taken in the early 1960s, shows a typical bunch. The locomotive interest is provided by 'Warship' class diesel-hydraulic, No D818 *Glory* and 'Modified Hall' No 6979 *Helperly Hall*.
C. J. Blay

in gas lighting when a new system of gas illumination was tried out on the advertising hoardings. Apparently the experiment was successful enough for it to be retained at Reading until the early 1950s. During 1938 the Great Western proudly announced proposals for the rebuilding of the station at Reading. Unfortunately the war intervened and the idea was shelved.

During the war Reading became a busy interchange point for many troops, and in August 1942 a new forces canteen with seating for 100 was opened at the station by Sir Felix Pole, who it is reported presented a wireless set for the forces use. The canteen which was paid for by the government, provided a 24hr service and was staffed by WVS personnel. After the war it was taken over by the Staff Association and is still in use today. The Great Western also constructed a new staff canteen at Reading. It was officially opened on 3 September 1943 by Sir James Milne. The two-storey building contained two dining rooms and had seating for 400 staff. Situated adjacent to the signal works in Caversham Road, it provided a full 24hr service of hot meals. For a number of years it was used as a

staff hostel and after some years out of use was demolished during 1984.

The station underwent a name change in November 1949 when the suffix 'General' was added. During 1955 the platforms at Reading were renumbered, with the west end bays becoming platforms 1, 2 and 3, the down main platform 4, the up main No 5, the down relief No 8, the east and west bays No 6 and 7 respectively, and the up relief and bay platforms Nos 9 and 10. Under the 1955 modernisation plan it had been proposed that the General station should be rebuilt. The plans which had been drawn up during 1960 showed a new down platform loop, together with a new concrete and glass booking office on the down-side platform. In 1962, and shortly before the work was due to start, the government announced that because of financial constraints it had shelved the plan.

The next major alteration to the station was a direct result of the closure of Reading Southern in September 1965. This saw the completion of a new electrified bay platform for the Waterloo services at the eastern end of platform 4. Designated number 4A, it was built on the site of a small parcels bay that

Above:
'Manor' No 7817 *Garsington Manor* stands on station pilot duty in East bay (platform 6) at Reading in May 1963. *D. Tuck*

had previously been unnumbered. Also about this time the 'General' suffix was dropped from the station name. Platform 4A was extended during 1975 by the addition of a second platform face. Numbered 4B, it was brought into use on 4 May 1975 for the newly inaugurated Gatwick services. On 26 April 1965 the Reading MAS scheme came into operation and from this date a new power box situated on the north side of the station took over the work of some 42 manual boxes in its area, with most if not all of the semaphore signals locally being removed. At the same time the up through line was reversibly signalled to allow two-way working for fast non-stop trains. This currently has a line speed of 80mph in either direction. In 1968 Reading won, for the very first time, the Western Region's best-kept station award, narrowly beating Newport. Charles Spencer the Deputy Area Manager received the award of a shield and a £50 cheque from David Pattison the Western Region London Divisional Manager.

In 1985, some 25 years after it was first mooted, it was decided to modernise the facilities at Reading. This £20 million venture was financed partially with the sale of railway land for office and warehouse development and partially by the InterCity sector. Work was started on 1 July 1986 with Mayoress Janet Bond cutting the first sod. What was left of the old Southern station was swept away and on its site was constructed a large office block, known as the Apex Plaza, and a new station entrance complex, the 'Brunel Arcade' which is linked to the Plaza. The new complex includes a shopping arcade as well as a ticket office, travel centre and a new Rail-Air transfer lounge. On the north side of the station the land vacated by the closure of the Vastern Road goods yard and signal works has been redeveloped into an industrial estate that includes a new 70,000sq ft postal sorting office, as well as a new multi-storey car park. The car park together with the new station arcade are directly connected to the station by way of a new walkway, with escalator access to the platforms. The whole complex was opened by Her Majesty the Queen on 4 April 1989, and now gives Reading a station which should see it well into the next century. The original Great Western building, which is grade two listed, has been restored and is now used for office accommodation.

Signalling at Reading

The earliest mention of any form of signalling at Reading, indeed on the Great Western itself, appears in Gooch's Regulations for the engines working trains to Reading on or after 30 March 1840. The final paragraph states: 'A signal ball will be seen at the entrance to Reading station when the line is right for the train to go in. If the ball is not visible the train must not pass it.' It does appear however that this ball type signal may well have been in use from the opening of the line in 1837. The first signal cabins did not appear at Reading until about 1874 as prior to this a system of ground signalling was in operation. In this system points and signals were operated by levers which were placed outdoors at various positions around the station yards, and no form of interlocking was provided. Trains arriving at Reading were dealt with by three sets of switchmen, each set controlled their individual 'beats' and each beat had their own small sentry hut for shelter. One of these at Reading was apparently so small that during the winter months the 'fire devil' (a form of heating stove) had to be placed outside. An amusing story is told regarding one of the switchmen who was found to be asleep in his hut by the local inspector. On discovery the man denied being asleep but when it was put to him that the inspector had seen his eyes shut, he remarked back, 'Why, it's so cold in this old box I was obliged to close my eyes to keep them warm!' These switchmen wandered around the yard setting the various points in their beats as the traffic required. The sentry huts at Reading were positioned at the eastern end of the station on the Vastern Road bridge, a second 'middle' hut stood in the centre of the station and a third, west hut, stood to the west of the Caversham Road bridge. It is interesting to note that when the signalboxes were built at Reading they were placed in the same positions as the old huts. The lack of any form of telegraph meant that the switchmen were relying almost solely on the trains running to time. Each switchman was supplied with a warning handbell and a clock, and the method relied heavily on their ability to remember which trains they had dealt with. This rather happy-go-lucky method of signalling at Reading is well described by Henry Ralph in his book *Railway Days and Railway Ways*:

'Five minutes before a down passenger was due, the east end man, if his end was clear, rang his handbell to call attention, at the same time exhibiting a white flag to the middle man; if he, the middle man, was clear he in turn would repeat that process to the west man. If he was clear he could walk round and set the points in his beat correctly. This done, he would exhibit a white flag to the middle man, who in turn would do a like duty and then turn his disc and cross-bar stop signal for the down line to "all right", seeing which, the east man having no points to manipulate for this road, would pull off his distant and then the home signal and wait for the train. No up train or branch train could be admitted beyond the home signal for those lines, unless it was an up through train, until the down train had arrived and was clear of all intersecting lines.'

At this time there were only three signals for each of the three through lines. Obviously one lapse of concentration from any of the switchmen could easily cause a serious accident. On one such occasion a switchman who was obviously tired, mistook the up 'Flying Dutchman' for a stopping train and diverted it into the platform road at some 55mph, spreading the passengers' luggage, which at this time was still carried on the top of the coaches, all over the platforms. It appears that this was not an isolated incident and it was probably only the stability of the broad gauge that prevented what could well have been a series of major accidents.

A block telegraph system of signalling was introduced between Southall and Goring in 1870. Under this system the line was divided into sections with a telegraph instrument at each block post. These were then used by the 'signalmen' to send line clear or train on line information to each adjacent section. As already mentioned, signal cabins with locking frames were first introduced at Reading in 1874 and corresponded in both name and position to the old sentry huts. Prior to the rebuilding of the station, cabins were situated at East Main Line, Middle and West Main Line. The East and Middle cabins were subsequently removed during the construction work on the new station. By the turn of the century, lines through the station at Reading were being controlled by various signalboxes. At Kennet Bridge (eight levers), a small box was opened during 1899 and controlled the eastern approaches to the station. The Main Line East Box (115 levers) was opened during 1896, and was situated on the London side of the Vastern Road bridge. This was a large box, measuring approximately 82ft × 15ft and it controlled the eastern end of the station, together with the junction to the South Eastern & Chatham lines. The original box here had been opened in 1874 and was situated to the west of the Vastern Road bridge. The entrance to signal works and low level yards was controlled by the High Level ground Frame (13 levers). This was situated alongside the incline on the north western side of the Vastern Road bridge. Alongside the low level incline and adjacent to the station stood Goods Lines East. This 57-lever box was opened during 1898 but was closed in 1923, when much of its work was switched to the other boxes in the area. The largest box at Reading, Main Line West (185 levers), was also the largest mechanical box on the whole of the system. It had been opened in 1896 as a direct replacement for an earlier box that stood on the same site. The new box, which measured 102ft × 15ft, was built in red brick, relieved by buff coloured bands, and its roof was decorated with cock's comb roof tiles and fleur-de-lys finials. Main Line West controlled the nearby Berks & Hants Junction. The junction itself underwent remodelling work during 1912 and as part of this work, Main Line West box was enlarged. Work started on 11 February, when the old 185-lever frame was dismantled. The installation of the new frame commenced the following day and took about a week to complete. The new frame was a four tier tappet-type, containing 208 levers with 14 spares, and was the largest ever produced at the nearby signal works. It weighed over 100 tons and had to be supported by a massive iron girder structure that

ran the length of the box. During the same year a new Middle box was opened at the west end of the up relief platform. It contained 21 levers and replaced a 10-lever ground frame that had been in use since the old Middle box was closed. The new box controlled shunting operations in connection with up and down relief passenger trains. Other boxes at Reading were situated at Goods Line West (43 levers), Reading West Junction (101 levers) and Scours Lane Junction (27 levers). During 1915 the latter two boxes had their frames extended to 134 and 39 levers respectively. The 1880 Ordnance Survey map also shows a box at Cow Lane, but the only details discovered about it are that it closed about 1910, probably to allow for the construction of the new down yard, and that it was subsequently

Below:
The crew of 'Bulldog' No 3386 *Paddington* pose proudly alongside their locomotive. In the background is the large box at Reading Main Line East. *Author's collection*

Right:
The interior of Main Line West signalbox. With its 222-lever frame, this was the largest mechanical box on the Great Western and later the Western Region. It was closed on 26 April 1965, but not finally demolished until August 1988. *Brian Davis collection*

Below right:
The little-photographed Reading Middle box, was opened in 1912 and contained a 21-lever frame. It was finally closed on 6 June 1959. *G. A. Carpenter collection*

69

replaced by a ground frame of the same name that stood in the new up yard. The ground frame appears to have been removed some time around 1925.

On the Berks & Hants there were just two boxes locally. The box at Oxford Road Junction (26 levers) was opened in 1906, and controlled both the junction and the signals at the adjacent Reading West station. The second box was at Southcote Junction, and this was fitted with a 34-lever frame and controlled the triple junction of the Berks & Hants, Basingstoke, and Central Goods lines. The small yard at Central Goods was itself controlled by a three-lever ground frame. During 1908 Automatic Train Control was fitted on all four tracks between Slough and Reading, with ramps being laid at all distance signals. It was extended from Slough to Paddington in 1910, but surprisingly not westwards from Reading until 1929.

During World War 2 several alterations were made locally. The construction of a new power station at Earley, together with new exchange sidings, saw the box at Sonning enlarged by the addition in June 1941 of a new 54-lever frame. During the same year a new spur junction was opened to the east of Reading to connect to the Southern lines. To avoid building a new box here, the nearby East Main was fitted with a new miniature 36-lever power frame, complete with

Above:
This picture, taken on 10 June 1964, shows the fine assortment of signals at the western end of Reading station. *Great Western Trust*

Above right:
The large signal gantry at the west end of Reading station is seen to good effect, as No 5001 *Llandovery Castle* passes through with a race special to Newbury. *C. J. Blay*

Right:
Railways at Reading circa 1955.

all electric interlocking. All the points and signals at the junction were also electrically operated.

After the war the existing boxes continued to give good service and during 1948 the box at Scours Lane was fitted with a new 52 level frame. Rationalisation during the late 1950s and early 1960s saw the closure of some of the boxes locally. Reading Middle box was closed on 6 June 1959, and on 13 February 1961 the boxes at Woodley Bridge and Sonning became surplus to requirements when their work was transferred to a new electric panel, fitted in Main Line East.

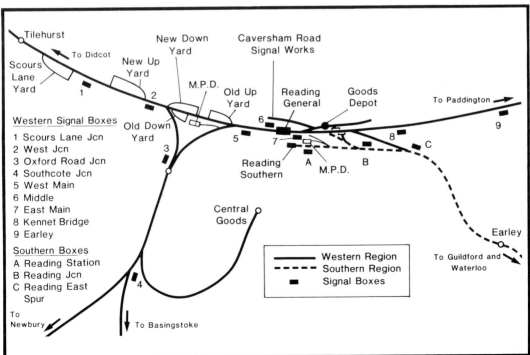

Tilehurst

To Didcot

Scours
Lane
Yard

New Down
Yard

New Up
Yard

M.P.D.

Old Up
Yard

Caversham Road
Signal Works

Reading
General

Goods
Depot

To Paddington

1

2

Old Down
Yard

6

9

Western Signal Boxes

1 Scours Lane Jcn
2 West Jcn
3 Oxford Road Jcn
4 Southcote Jcn
5 West Main
6 Middle
7 East Main
8 Kennet Bridge
9 Earley

3

5

7

Reading
Southern

A

Reading
M.P.D.

B

8

C

Southern Boxes

A Reading Station
B Reading Jcn
C Reading East
   Spur

Central
Goods

Earley

To Guildford and
Waterloo

4

To
Newbury

To Basingstoke

Western Region
Southern Region
Signal Boxes

In 1955 the Western Region had announced its Modernisation Plan, with the proposal to completely re-signal the Western Region, using new power boxes together with multiple-aspect signalling. By the 1960s the new signalling scheme was progressing along the old Great Western main line with new power boxes being opened at Old Oak Common and Slough. In 1965 the Reading area was completed with the opening of a new central power box at

Reading on 26 April 1965. On the same day all existing manual boxes in the area were closed. The new power box initially controlled an area of 64 route and 184 track miles and replaced 42 manual boxes. The saving in manpower was enormous, for the new box required only four signalmen plus one standby per shift. In 1972 its control was extended even further, when it took over the work of the remaining manual boxes at Twyford and Henley. Once closed, many of the old boxes were soon swept away, but the grandest of them all, Main Line West, remained *in situ,* albeit an empty shell, until it was demolished during 1988. Incredibly, Goods Line East, which was closed in the 1920s continued to be used as a store, and was not finally demolished until 1987. At the time of writing, Goods Line West is still standing and is currently used as a store for the nearby engineering section.

Above:
Main Line West signalbox circa 1960. *C. J. Blay*

Below:
The new power signalbox at Reading, pictured here in April 1965, shortly after being commissioned.
British Rail

The Great Western Signal Works

Tucked away and almost out of sight from the rail traveller, at a lower level alongside the Great Western station, stood a group of small buildings in which for many years almost all of the signalling equipment used on the Great Western Railway was produced. This was the Reading Signal Works.

Signals as such were not used on the Great Western until the line was opened through to Reading during 1840. Prior to this individual sections of the line from Paddington to Maidenhead were patrolled by policemen. In 1841 Brunel had introduced his disc and crossbar signals, which were constructed and maintained by outside contractors. The first mention of a separate signal works does not appear until about 1859. Before this date both the permanent way and fixed signals had been maintained by district contractors. It appears that the GWR took over the plant of one of these contractors that had been situated at Slough, and set up their own central repair works at Reading, on land adjacent to both the station and Caversham Road. Initially the work was undertaken in one small shed, using just a handful of men who were under the control of Mr Thomas Blackall, the first manager of the works. A separate repair shop nearby also dealt with the repairs to the engineering department's wagons. Other work such as the construction of footbridges, cranes and permanent way equipment was also undertaken on this site. The first semaphore signals to be built at Reading were erected between Paddington and Kensal Green and became operational on 1 April 1865.

The signal works were only able to meet a small proportion of the requirements at this time and many of the early boxes were constructed by either Saxby & Farmer or McKensie, Clunes & Holland, but gradual expansion at Reading allowed the Great Western's own signal department, which by 1872 was employing some 500 men, to undertake the bulk of the work. In 1872 the first interlocking frame was constructed at Reading, for use at Taplow. The locking mechanism of this frame was made to the requirements of Michael Lane (Chief Engineer to the Great Western between 1860 and 1868). The design of the frame is reputed to have been the work of John Gooderson, the foreman of the fitting shop, although A. T. Blackall claimed in a paper to The Institute of Civil Engineers in 1911, that it was designed by his father.

Disaster struck on the evening of 19 December 1874, when a severe fire destroyed many of the old buildings. The fire had started in a timber storehouse and, with the fire fighting apparatus proving to be inadequate, it soon engulfed the rest of the buildings. The following report from the *Berkshire Chronicle* of 26 December 1874 describes the fire:

'The Great Western Railway iron works were destroyed by fire on Saturday. At half past two this morning the alarm of a fire was raised when it was discovered that the GW Railway works situated in the Caversham Road, Reading, were on fire. The borough engines were soon on the spot and were quickly followed by the county engine and Messrs Suttons' engine. By the time the engines were got ready and water obtained, the fire had laid hold of nearly the whole of the block of buildings and was burning furiously, and despite the strenuous exertions made by the police, the fire brigade and the help given by the public it was seen that any efforts to save the buildings would be useless, and the efforts of the firemen were more directed towards saving the carpenter's shop attached to the works and Mr Hood's foundry. It originated in the north-east corner of the buildings, but the cause of it is not yet known. At the time of going to press the fire, though partially subdued was still raging. The buildings with the exception of the carpenter's shop are completely destroyed. The conflagration was witnessed by hundreds of people. It is estimated that it will throw between four and five hundred hands out of work.'

Another report notes that 'no one knew where the hydrants were in the works and had they been found, they were too small to supply the large borough engine'. One of the most unfortunate consequences of the fire, from an historical point of view, was the destruction of many of the early records of the signal department.

The works were subsequently rebuilt, and the wagon repair section together with some of the other operations were switched away to Swindon and other locations, thereby leaving much of the remaining site for signal production and maintenance. However, some of the permanent way work, notably the manufacture of points and crossings continued here until 1902, after which date this work was also moved away to Swindon. During 1885 Thomas Blackall was promoted to become the company's first Chief Signal Engineer, and during April of the same year production at Reading had reached such a level that the GWR issued the following notice: 'All new signalling and locking gear will in future be constructed at Reading by Mr Blackall. The Divisional Engineer will maintain all existing signals and lockings. No existing signals or locking to be made or altered except from tables supplied by Mr Blackall and approved by the General Manager and Superintendent of the line.'

Thomas Blackall retired in 1893, but his son A. T. Blackall, who had joined the company during 1879, was appointed Assistant in Charge at Reading. Also during 1893 all signalling maintenance work on the Great Western was transferred from the engineering section to the signalling department. Between Blackall's retirement in 1893 and the appointment of his son, the works were under the control of the Locomotive Superintendent, William Dean. Extensive flooding took place at Reading during November 1894 and the whole of the Caversham Road area, including the office block and workshop, was under 2ft of water. In 1897 A. T. Blackall was promoted to become the Chief Signal Engineer, thereby following in his father's footsteps. During August of the same

year overall responsibility for the signal department within the company was transferred to the General Manager. On 27 July 1903 the signalling and telegraph departments were amalgamated, and the signal works was once again extended by the construction of a new telegraph shop, offices and stores. These housed the 397 staff of the telegraph section that were transferred to Reading from the old telegraph offices at Westbourne Park.

The *Great Western Magazine* states that between 1896 and 1910 the works were turning out on average some 150 signalboxes per year. In 1912 a new locking frame containing 174 working levers and 34 spares was finished; it was the largest to be constructed in the works, and was fitted during February into the Main Line West signalbox at Reading. The old 185-lever frame that was removed from the box, had up to that point been the largest frame constructed at Reading. During 1921 the maintenance and repair of the company clocks and watches was transferred to a new clock shop, which was established within the signal works. Prior to this, repairs were undertaken by private contractors, notably Kays of Worcester. The 'clock shop' at Reading had for many years a staff of 13; these were

74

75

responsible for the repair and maintenance of some 5,500 watches, 4,500 station and office clocks and 3,500 brass drum timepieces. Each timepiece was given its own record card, and on average this small but important department had a repair output of about 120 timepieces a week.

The signal works, at this time, covered an area of some eight acres and contained 19 separate repair shops, together with a drawing office. Extensive sidings gave access to the erecting shops and the stores department warehouses. Power was supplied via two separate power houses. Engine House **(1)** contained an auxiliary 70hp steam engine fed from two ex-locomotive boilers, each working alternately. The boilers also provided steam for the steam hammers in the smith's shop and also for heating the general offices. A second Power House **(2)** contained a more powerful 120hp engine which, like Engine House **(1)** was fed by two ex-locomotive boilers. This engine was the older of the two, and was apparently constructed soon after the opening of the works. Both engines were fed by injectors with soft water from the water softening plant at the locomotive depot.

An interesting glimpse into the amount of equipment being maintained by the signalling department can be found in the 1923 *Great Western Magazine* which lists particulars of signalling equipment in use at that time. This comprised: 2,066 Signalboxes; 23,467 Signals; 58,680 Working Levers; 14,456 Points; 4,824 Facing point locking sets; 11,025 Independent discs; 683 Ground Frames; 354 Level Crossing gates: 419 Weighted fouling bars;

2,014 Detonator-placing machines; 942 Track circuits; 581 Electrically worked signals; 12,000 Telephones; 35,902 Long burning lamps; 9,800 Portable Accumulators; 3,050 Clocks and 4 Accumulator Charging Depots, charging 65,000 accumulators per year'. The signalling maintenance staff at this time comprised some 2,510 employees, of which 322 were actually employed at the signal works.

The works saw further expansion after the Grouping when the department took over responsibility for the many smaller lines which had now become part of the Great Western. In June 1923 A. T. Blackall retired, to be succeeded by R. J. S. Insell, and improvements continued at Reading, with a new design of interlocking frame going into production during the same year. Records for 1925 show the manufacture during that year of some 70 interlocking frames, totalling 1,098 levers, 20 complete new boxes, 132 wooden signals, 285 concrete signals and one complete gantry. Insell unfortunately died in March 1928, and was succeeded by C. M. Jacobs who continued as signal engineer until his retirement in February 1936. He was succeeded during the same month by F. H. D. Page. A report by the signal engineer dated December 1931 mentions that during the year the signal department removed 26 redundant boxes and erected 13 new ones.

In October 1946 the Great Western announced that the signal works were to be modernised at a cost of some £300,000, and although some preliminary work was started during the following year, the bulk of the work was held in abeyance until after Nationalisation. The signalling engineer's job had changed hands once again in April 1947 when Page retired and was succeeded by A. W. Woodbridge, and it was he who had the task of taking the works into the British Railways era. It is worth mentioning that soon after Nationalisation, a proposal was put forward by the newly formed British Railways Board to standardise all the semaphore signals throughout the country. This meant that the lower quadrant Western Region signals would have to be converted into upper quadrants. This suggestion apparently horrified the Western S&T department, who were all of course still firmly Great Western men. It appears that in order to appease the board, an 'experimental' upper quadrant signal was constructed at Reading and erected for a trial period

Left:
The main stamping shop circa 1923. *Author's collection*

Below:
This interesting picture shows the signal works display inside the town hall at Reading circa 1947. The occasion appears to be an exhibition of local trades, put on in collaboration with the National Savings movement.
Great Western Trust

at Oxford North Junction during December 1950. The subsequent proposals for the modernisation of the Western Region saw the whole idea dropped, although the 'experimental' signal stayed in operation at Oxford until 1973!

Woodbridge's time at Reading was not without incident for on the evening of 26 January 1950 the works once again caught fire. The blaze, although severe, was luckily confined to a 50-year-old timber store and carpenter's shop. The fire had actually started in an electrical assembly shop, which because of reconstruction work was situated on the top floor of the old drying shed. With the fire station being situated almost opposite the works, in Caversham Road, assistance was immediate. The outbreak, however, took over an hour to bring under control, the shed being completely destroyed. It was obvious that this hotch-potch of old buildings needed renewing and during the same year, under the direction of the Signal & Telegraph section, a start was once again made on the modernisation of the works. This required the rebuilding of the S&T workshops and the incorporation within its structure of a new stores and workshop complex. Work was finally finished during March 1952. The new

stores building had a total floor area of about 50,000sq ft, almost trebling the storage capacity of the various small buildings that it replaced. Although many of the smaller buildings were swept away to make room for the new stores, the main building of the old stores was retained and subsequently used as a training school for the S&T department. The clock & watch section was also provided with a new modern workshop, situated within the north-east corner of the new building. During the 2½ years of rebuilding work the clock & watch department continued to operate from a disused signalbox in the works yard. A. W. Woodbridge retired in 1959 and was replaced by Armand Cardani. It had been invisaged soon after Nationalisation that the signal works at Reading would be expanded to produce both mechanical boxes and signals for the whole of British Railways, but this proposal was dropped once the decision had been made to modernise the system using electric panel boxes. By the early 1960s the work of the signal department had changed somewhat. With the Modernisation Plan in full swing, the old mechanical boxes were being gradually replaced by the new electric panel boxes, using power equipment manufactured by the Westinghouse & General Signal Co. The signal works now performed a role of maintenance only, with no mechanical frames of note being built, although the construction of signals, posts and gantries continued. In 1965 the works underwent a partial rationalisation, and this resulted in some 13,000sq ft space being given over to use by the BR HQ for the accommodation of the Reading computer bureau.

In 1968 Cardani retired and was replaced by Maurice Leach, the last GWR home-grown man. On 16 November 1970, following a major departmental re-organisation, the S&T headquarters were transferred from Caversham Road to Western Tower. The offices at Caversham Road were subsequently occupied by the BR Business systems division. By 1973 the workforce had dropped to about 70 with another 20 or so in the stores. Many of the former were now employed on the overhaul of point machines, as well as on the production of clamp locks, level crossing barriers, ground frames and lineside cupboards, of which some 1,200 a year were being produced. The clock department was still receiving about 60 clocks and watches a week for repair, but by now its workforce had dropped to just six men and one foreman. During 1983 a decision was taken to move the signal works in order to release the land, which by now had become a

Below:

The Reading Signal & Telegraph Engineer's inspection saloon, No KDW150266, seen alongside the old East Goods box at Reading on 24 October 1985. The coach was formerly Collett RCO No W5440 built to diagram H33 on lot No 1349 in 1925. It was converted to signal department use in 1960. *B. Davis*

valuable asset, for other uses. A new site was found nearby at Woodley Airfield, using a hangar in which Spitfires had once been built. The old Caversham Road works finally closed it doors for the last time on 29 June 1984.

Signal Engineers at Reading

T. Blackall	1885-1893
A. T. Blackall	1897-1923
R. J. Insell	1923-1928
C. M. Jacobs	1928-1936
F. H. D. Page	1936-1947
A. W. Woodbridge	1947-1959
A. A. Cardani	1959-1969
M. Leach	1969-1974
R. Brown	1974-1977
F. Kerr	1977-1989
P. Wing	1989-

Note:

Between June 1893 and August 1897 the signal department was under the direct control of W. Dean at Swindon.

Below:

The new signal works machine shop at Woodley airfield, July 1985. *B. Davis*

Signal Works Locomotives

In order to move many of the heavy materials both in and out of the works, various shunting locomotives were allocated specifically to this duty over the years.

The first Signal Works locomotive appears to have been the former Whitland & Cardigan 0-6-0ST No 3. Built in 1877, it was taken into GW stock during September 1886 and renumbered 1387. In June 1900 it was withdrawn from general service and allocated to the signal works, where it continued to work until being replaced in February 1926 by a new Simplex 0-4-0 petrol shunting locomotive works No 3820. This was subsequently numbered 27 by the GWR in November 1932. The passing years saw the Simplex become increasingly unreliable, with constant breakdowns. It seems that during the 1950s the situation was particularly bad, with the Simplex spending longer periods away at Swindon. At these times other motive power was drafted in to fill the gap. In 1950, for example, GW 0-6-0ST No 1925 took over for several weeks, whilst in April 1953 ex-Powlesland & Mason 0-4-0ST No 1153 was used. The steam engines, it seems, were not popular replacements as they apparently filled the shops with smoke and fumes. By 1957 it was obvious that the Simplex had seen its best days, and it was replaced during the same year by a Ruston & Hornsby chain-driven 0-4-0DM No 20. The Simplex lay derelict in the signal works yards for a number of years before being officially withdrawn in July 1960.

In the 1970s No 20 was renumbered into departmental stock as No 97020, and in April 1981 it was replaced by ex-Dumfermline-based Andrew Barclay 0-4-0DM No 06003. With the closure of the works on 26 June 1984, this became the last works shunter.

Mention must also be made of 2-4-0T No 1299, as although it did not work in the signal works, it did work for many years in the nearby engineering yard. No 1299 started life as South Devon Railway 2-4-0ST *Jupiter*. It was partially constructed at Newton Abbot works, but due to the amalgamation of that company with the GWR, was completed at Swindon as a side tank in December 1878. It was numbered 1299 by the Great Western and fitted with a crane in April 1881, and in June was transferred to the engineering department at Reading. It continued to work here until it was transferred back into capital stock in June 1893.

Locomotive Depots

The Great Western Shed

The first locomotive shed provided by the Great Western Railway at Reading was opened during November 1840, some eight months after the railway arrived at Reading. For these first eight months locomotives were serviced at a temporary engine house which was situated at the western arch of the Kennet River bridge. No other details of this temporary shed can be found. The first 'permanent' shed contained two roads, each capable of holding up to four locomotives. It stood adjacent to the station and was constructed of brick and stone and carried large water tanks within its gable-styled slated roof. The building at this time measured approximately 160ft × 45ft. At the west end there were two short sidings, one for hay and straw traffic and the other for locomotive coal. In October 1861 one road of the shed was converted to mixed gauge, and at the same time the two sidings were given over to locomotive department usage. This extra room allowed the old building to be enlarged into a through shed, by the addition of a pair of wooden flat-roofed extensions. These were placed at either end of the original shed, and each measured

approximately 27ft × 45ft. A 45ft turntable stood to the east, with coaling and water facilities provided at the west end. During October 1864 the mixed gauge road at the shed was lengthened at a cost of £40. With its cramped position it was obvious that the shed would have to be replaced at some stage. Surprisingly this was not done until 1880, when a new roundhouse-type shed was constructed approximately ½ mile away, within the triangle of lines to the west of the station.

It is worth mentioning that a proposal had been made as early as 1865 to replace the locomotive shed with a larger structure. It was also suggested that the old shed might be reused possibly at Weymouth, but this was never undertaken. Certainly during broad gauge days the old shed was probably quite

Below:
This fine view shows the east yard at Reading shed in 1921. Locomotives on view include, from left to right, 'County' class 4-4-0 No 3810 *County Wicklow*, 'Bulldog' 4-4-0s Nos 3407 *Madras* and 3386 *Paddington*. Notice also the incredible yard gas lamp. *Great Western Trust*

adequate for the local needs as the regular allocation here rarely rose above 12 locomotives. Even at this time, some Reading locomotives were being out-stabled. From December 1847 at Hungerford, where a small two-road shed and turntable was provided, a Reading saddle tank was usually outstabled here until the closure of that shed in November 1862. From November 1848 a Reading locomotive was kept at Basingstoke, although a shed was not built here until 1850. The allocation list for 1860 shows Reading locomotives at Henley, Hungerford, Wycombe, Basingstoke and Taplow. As already mentioned, during 1880 a new partially mixed gauge shed was opened to the west of Reading and within the triangle of lines formed by the west and east loops. The old broad gauge shed was subsequently reused by the goods department.

The new Great Western shed at Reading was constructed of brick with a slate roof and was formed into three bays. The whole building measured 210ft × 150ft, and contained within its walls a roundhouse. Central to this was a 45ft turntable with one through road via the turntable and 17 radiating bays, one of which also formed a second exit from the shed. A short single dead-end road also ran into the shed from the eastern end. This layout gave a total storage space of about 945ft. A small single road lifting shop measuring approximately 90ft × 30ft was also contained within the walls, although this may well have been a later addition. In 1895 a small brick-built boilerhouse was constructed alongside the lifting shop. The shed water tank with a capacity of 37,500gal was situated to the south of the shed. It is very unlikely that mixed gauge trackwork was extended into the roundhouse area, and it is possible that the single dead-end road into the shed was used for housing

the few broad gauge locomotives which were still left at Reading at this time. Adjacent to the west end of the shed stood a wooden carriage shed, which contained five roads and measured approximately 200ft × 75ft. It was removed during the yard alterations of 1900. A coal stage, also constructed of wood, was situated to the east of the site. It was subsequently rebuilt during 1883 using corrugated iron, but this structure did not survive for long, as in 1900 alterations were undertaken to improve the overall layout of the depot. One of these alterations was the provision of a new coal stage. Constructed of brick, it was situated to the west of the shed building in the newly-extended yard. Repairs were undertaken on the shed roof during 1904, and in June 1905, after years of complaint about the poor standard of water at the shed (the water was obtained from the nearby Kennet), the Great Western installed a water softening plant, which was situated alongside the shed water tank. The new plant had a supply capacity of 15,000gal per hour. In order to accommodate the increasing size of Great Western locomotives, a new, larger 65ft undergirder turntable, which was fully boarded over, was constructed in the extended yard at the west end of the shed during January 1914. Also around this time some alterations were made to the track layout inside the roundhouse. This produced a much more rational layout with the number of turntable bays being increased to 20.

Reading was now becoming an increasingly busy shed, and to improve both accessibility and servicing facilities, new proposals were put forward by the Great Western during 1929 for the 'improvement of the engine shed at Reading'. One interesting proposal was to construct a second new roundhouse building utilising the 65ft turntable. After much

Left:
'481' class 2-4-0 No 481, built at Swindon in 1869, pictured inside the roundhouse at Reading at around the turn of the century. This particular locomotive was withdrawn in July 1912, but No 487, the last survivor of the class, was withdrawn from Reading in March 1921. *L&GRP*

Right:
This view of Collett 0-6-0 No 2253 shows to good effect the large shed water-softening plant which was installed at Reading in June 1905. *L&GRP*

Below:
This view of the locomotive shed at Reading was taken on 12 October 1921. The original lifting shop can be seen just to the right of the water-softening plant. The fence in the foreground is constructed in true Great Western fashion, out of old boiler tubes. *Great Western Trust*

Top left:
'County' class 4-6-0 No 1004 *County of Somerset* stands on the turntable at Reading on 21 June 1955.
Brian Morrison

Left:
In October 1961 the interior of the lifting shop at Reading has an unusual visitor in the form of 'King' class No 6027 *King Richard I*. *C. J. Blay*

Top:
This evocative picture shows No 6871 *Bourton Grange* removing the remaining steam locomotives, Nos 4919, 6966, 6107 and 6139, from the ex-GW shed at Reading on Sunday 3 January 1965. The shed had been officially closed to steam on the previous day.
Great Western Trust

Above:
'Remembrance' class 4-6-0 No 32329 *Stephenson* stands in the shed yard at Reading (81D) on 21 June 1955. Towards the end of their working life, members of this class saw regular use on the local services between Basingstoke and Reading. *Brian Morrison*

deliberation by the company this idea was abandoned, and it was decided instead to convert the existing roundhouse into a nine-road straight shed, with the minimum of external alteration, although the shed was completely re-roofed and glazed. The *Great Western Railway Magazine* of February 1930 carried the following notice: 'The existing engine shed at Reading is of the turntable type with one table and 20 radial roads. Improved accommodation is required and it is proposed, in connection with heavy maintenance repair work now necessary, to convert the shed into the straight-road type.' The majority of the work, which was undertaken by Bowyers of Slough, was completed by January 1932. Other improvements undertaken during the same period saw the provision in the east end locomotive yard of a new lifting and repair shop. It was built to the standard Great Western design for lifting shops, using a steel framework construction, clad on the outside with corrugated asbestos sheeting. The building measured 85ft × 40ft and contained a 50ton engine hoist manufactured by Royce of Manchester.

Alongside the north face of the shed, improved offices, stores and accommodation for the locomotive crews were provided. As with many other Great Western sheds, Reading saw further improvements during World War 2. Extra access roads to the turntable were provided, together with an extension to the coaling plant, which allowed a second coaling line to be laid to the north of the existing plant. This work was finally finished during 1943 and provided Reading with a much improved coaling capacity. A corrugated iron ash shelter was constructed in 1940 to cover the ash road adjacent to the turntable. Surprisingly, for many years there was a snowplough based at Reading, possibly an inheritance from the 1881 blizzards!

Nationalisation saw the shed recoded from the Great Western RDG to the new BR code of 81D. The shed itself changed little during the years after Nationalisation, although extensive renewal work was undertaken to the roof during the summer of 1956. By the late 1950s, however, it became apparent that the days of steam at Reading were numbered, with the proposal by the Western Region to construct a new diesel servicing depot. This was duly completed in August 1959. The three-track shed was initially used solely for servicing diesel shunters and diesel multiple-units. It was situated in the yard behind the steam depot on land

reclaimed by the removal of the steam depot coal stack and sidings. Extensive DMU stabling facilities, together with a refuelling bay, had been opened a few months earlier on the site of the old tip sidings, situated between the West of England main line and Reading west curve. In December 1963 it was announced that the diesel depot would be extended to provide servicing facilities for main line locomotives. The work was completed during 1964 with

Below:
The driver gives 'Modified Hall' No 7917 *North Aston Hall* **a final check prior to leaving the shed at Reading in June 1964.** *C. J. Blay*

Right:
The wonderful atmosphere of a steam shed is captured in this shot of the interior of Reading. The four locomotives on view are all members of the '6100' class and, although the photograph is undated, it was probably taken during the final months of steam at the shed. *B. Davis collection*

Below right:
Double chimney-fitted 'King' No 6026 *King John* **stands outside the lifting shop at Reading in June 1959. The locomotive was awaiting attention after apparently running a 'hot box'.** *Author's collection*

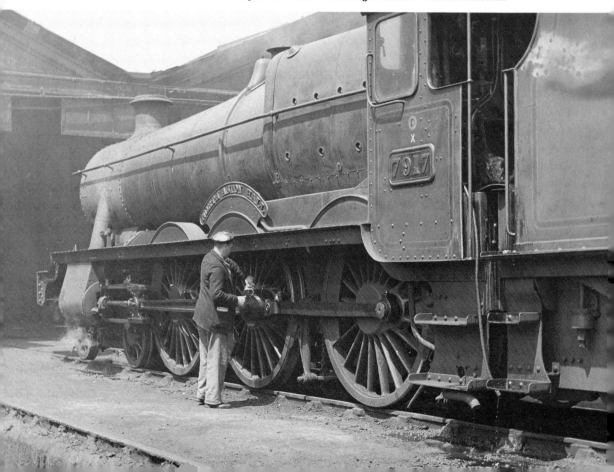

the provision of a 150ft long two-road extension to the DMU shed. The steam shed continued to be used, although it was gradually becoming more and more unkempt due to lack of maintenance, the roof in particular suffering badly. The end came on Saturday 2 January 1965 when the shed was finally closed to steam. The very last locomotive in steam to leave the shed was 'Grange' class No 6871 *Bourton Grange*, which left the following day hauling four condemned locomotives: Nos 4919 *Donnington Hall*,

6966 *Witchingham Hall* and Prairie tanks Nos 6107 and 6139.

Demolition of the shed building took place soon afterwards, and the site was then used for a number of years as additional siding space. In 1972 the PW depot at Theale was closed and moved to the site of the old steam shed. In 1981 the existing diesel depot was once again enlarged by the provision of a new building alongside the existing shed. This contained two additional tracks which now provided Reading with a five-road maintenance shed. Since 1986 the depot has been part of the Network SouthEast sector, providing maintenance levels of 2 for locomotives and 4 for DMUs.

The Southern Shed

When the Reading, Guildford & Reigate Railway finally inaugurated through services between Redhill and Reading on 15 October 1849, servicing at the Reading end was undertaken in a small yard, which stood adjacent to the single platform terminus

station. This 'loco yard' comprised nothing more than a pair of engine sidings, a water crane, and a 45ft turntable. Whatever coaling facilities there were, are not shown on early maps, and were probably provided direct from a wagon. It is also unclear whether these facilities were actually in use when the first section of the line to Farnborough had been opened in July of the same year.

The South Eastern Railway, which purchased the line from the Reading & Reigate during 1852 very soon afterwards constructed a two-road shed over

Top:
Wainwright 'D' No 31075 stands in the sun at Reading South on 10 May 1952. *J. B. Snell*

Above:
The SE&CR Reading Locomotive Department football team of the 1921-22 season left to right back: Unknown, J. Townsend, J. Hewett, A. Ayres, A. Billing, F. Bonney. Middle: W. Knight, T. Mudge, Mr Drake (Foreman), L. Manton, G. Eamer. Bottom: Unknown, F. Jones, B. Hockley, Unknown. *Courtesy Jack Hewett*

the site of the locomotive sidings and adjacent to the turntable. Constructed in brick and stone with a slate roof, the open-ended shed measured 110ft × 38ft. During the 1860s the yard here was extensively remodelled, with the small two-road shed being replaced by a new and much larger three-road shed. This was situated on the opposite side of the running lines, and adjacent to the embankment of the GWR main line. Once the new shed was opened, the old building was not removed but saw further use, firstly as a goods depot and in later years as part of a bonded warehouse. It survived in this guise, sandwiched between a pair of later extensions, until its demolition in the early 1970s. It is also worth mentioning that the siding that once served the old turntable was known as the 'table road' right up until the closure of the yard. The new shed, designated No 18 by the SECR,

contained three roads and was constructed of brick with a pitched slated roof; the whole structure measured 150ft × 56ft. Wooden doors were provided at the Vastern Road end of the shed but these were removed soon after the end of World War 1, thus leaving the shed open at both ends. Photographic evidence suggests that at some point around the turn of the century the shed roof was extensively rebuilt. A 45ft turntable stood at the eastern end of the yard. It is possible that this was the original 1849 turntable re-sited. It was subsequently replaced during 1926 with a new 65ft diameter table. Other alterations completed at the same time saw the provision of an improved coal stage, at the rear of the shed.

The water here was obviously no better than the nearby GW shed, for in 1941 the Southern Railway installed a water softening plant, adjacent to one of the turntable roads. At the same time some improvements were made to the coaling plant and yard layout. Little subsequent physical alteration took place to the shed, which after Nationalisation was coded 70E by the Southern Region. On 10 May 1954 Reading South effectively lost its independent status and most of its locomotives were reallocated to Redhill and Guildford, the latter undertaking the administration of Reading from then on. This was a strange decision as Reading continued to retain its own shed code, and for a number of years still maintained an allocation of two small tank locomotives for yard and pilot duties. Other motive power, however, was now mainly provided by these two sheds. Stranger still was the announcement in 1962 (after some eight years of being administered

Left:
A view of the rear yard at Reading South shows Reading South signalbox. The original South Eastern locomotive shed (arched windows), can be seen in the centre of the bonded warehouse. *R. Ruffell*

Below left:
Members of the footplate staff relax in the mess room at Reading South. *R. Ruffell*

Below:
Possibly one of the last steam engines to use the facilities at Reading South was 'N' class No 31866, pictured on 21 August 1965. A 'Crompton' Class 33 can also be seen, inside the shed. *R. Ruffell*

by Guildford), that Reading was now officially its sub-shed. In this guise the shed building continued in use to both house and service steam locomotives until its official closure on 6 April 1964, although the yard and turntable continued to see occasional use right up until the end of steam traction on the Reading branch. Once steam had gone, the shed building, although derelict, remained basically intact; it was finally demolished during the first two weeks of December 1965. For many years Reading also maintained a small two road brick-built sub-shed at Ash. It was opened in 1856, and generally up to four locomotives were outstabled here. The shed was officially closed in 1946; the building, however, survived and is today used for industrial purposes. Over the years the number of men employed at the SE shed at Reading numbered around 100. Within this number were the locomotive crews, comprising between 36 and 45 sets of men, the higher figure being reached during the wars. The arrival of the electrics in 1939 saw 12 of these men switched from steam duties and trained especially for operating the new electric services to Waterloo. Even today there are still 30 drivers based at Reading for the operation of the Southern services, which now come under the jurisdiction of the area manager at Feltham.

The closure of the shed brought to a close the long association with the SECR at Reading of the Hewett family. Jack Hewett was the last shed foreman at Reading South, and had joined the railway in 1917,

Above:
The semi-derelict locomotive shed and yard at Reading South can be seen to good effect in this picture, taken from a 'Tadpole' unit as it arrives at Reading with service from Tonbridge, on 29 August 1965. *R. Ruffell*

Above right:
A sad sight for steam enthusiasts was the demolition of the Southern shed. This photograph, taken from the coal road on 11 December 1965, shows the task almost complete. *R. Ruffell*

Right:
The last foreman at Reading South was Jack Hewett, pictured here (third left) in 1964 with some members of his staff. *R. Ruffell*

first cleaning locomotives for his father, Driver John Hewett. John had started on the South Eastern at Reading in 1881, and died in service at the age of 64. Jack eventually became a driver, being based for most of his working life at Reading. He retired from railway service in 1966 and today lives not far from his favourite line at Earley. The story does not end there, for Jack also had two elder brothers, Michael and Harry, both of whom also became drivers for the SECR at Reading, entering service in 1911 and 1915 respectively. Their uncle, Alfred Beerling, who started in 1885 was also a driver here. This is quite a remarkable story of one family's service to the SECR at Reading.

Motive Power Summary

Great Western

Mention has already been made of the types of locomotives used for the opening of the line to Reading. These were initially kept and serviced in the roundhouse at Bishops Road (Paddington) and at the temporary engine house to the east of Reading. At this time (1840) it appears that locomotives worked between the two engine houses and were not in fact allocated to any specific one. By about 1845 this seems to have changed, and locomotives are shown in the Gooch Registers as working from specific 'stations'. It appears that this term was used to indicate an engine house. In 1850 for instance, 10 locomotives were shown at Reading, which apart from a solitary 0-6-0, were all either 2-2-2s or 2-4-0s of the 'Sun', 'Leo' or 'Priam' classes. A report dated November 1860 shows the distribution of Reading locomotives. The allocation comprised eight passenger, one goods and one ballast locomotives, of which six were at Reading, one at Henley, one at Hungerford and one at Wycombe, with the ballast engine working at Taplow.

By 1862 the total had increased to 12 with the addition of a pair of 'Premier' class 0-6-0 goods locomotives. It was around this time that the shed was mixed, and although it seems that there were no standard gauge classes actually allocated to Reading at this time, certainly examples of England 2-4-0s and Sharp and Gooch 0-6-0s would have been working in the area. As the standard gauge spread, services in the area were taken over by Armstrong 0-6-0 goods and 0-6-0 saddle tanks and, of course, the '517' class 0-4-2T. Many of the passenger services locally were in the hands of 'Cobham' and 'Sir Daniel' class 2-2-2s. A pair of 'River' class 2-4-0s, Nos 75 *Teign* and 76 *Wye*, were allocated to Reading for a number of years prior to the turn of the century, being used mainly for station pilot work. I can find no record of when, exactly, the last broad gauge locomotives were allocated to Reading, but it seems unlikely that there were any after about 1876, although as already mentioned, the new locomotive shed was for a time partially mixed.

Reading had many intermediate and branch turns and this was reflected in the allocation over the years. Certainly the construction of the new goods yards in 1880 saw the allocation of 0-6-0 tanks increase. By the turn of the century the allocation at Reading stood at 48, comprising no fewer than 18 different classes, of which 12 were 0-6-0 tank locomotives for yard shunting. Also of interest in the 1901 allocation was the ex-South Devon Railway 0-4-0ST No 1328, which was possibly at Reading for engineering department use.

Some of the secondary duties on the Berks & Hants line at this time were in the hands of '481' class 2-4-0s, of which a number were allocated to Reading. No 387, the last of the class, survived here until its withdrawal during March 1921. In May 1914 a pair of steam railmotors were allocated to Reading for the newly-introduced services to Henley-on-Thames and Basingstoke. During 1917 Reading also became responsible for supplying the motive power for the Lambourn Valley branch. This generally took the form of an '850' class 0-6-0T, but from about 1929 a pair of ex-M&SWJR 2-4-0s, Nos 1335 and 1336, were allocated to Reading specifically for this working.

By the 1920s the allocation contained many 4-4-0s of the 'Atbara', 'Flower', 'City', 'County' and 'Bulldog' classes. In 1925 the GWR purchased a number of ROD 2-8-0s, which were stored around the system before being taken to Swindon. Reading had three of these, Nos 3033, 3058 and 3098, for over a year. Gradually, however, the older classes at Reading, which included some ancient 2-4-0s, were phased out, many being replaced by the new Churchward Moguls, which by the end of the decade at Reading totalled 13. In 1927 the first 4-6-0 'Saint' No 2937 *Clevedon Court* was allocated to Reading. However, by 1930 this had departed, being replaced by fellow class members Nos 2926 *St Nicholas* and 2981 *Ivanhoe*. These in turn were replaced with members of the new 'Hall' class. These locomotives were obviously popular at Reading, for by the end of the decade there were 11 examples based here. A change of branch line motive power took place during December 1933 with the arrival of a pair of new '4800' class 0-4-2Ts, Nos 4827 and 4828, for the Henley and Wallingford services. These replaced '517' class No 458 and 'Metro' 2-4-0T No 1459, which were allocated away during the same month. In December 1934 the last steam railmotor at Reading, No 37, was withdrawn. Some of the old railmotor services were now taken over by the newly-introduced diesel railcars. Cars Nos 1, 12 and 18 were allocated to Reading to cover services to Henley, Slough and Newbury. Other changes at this

time saw the introduction during 1931 of the new Collett '6100' class 2-6-2Ts on to the semi-fast services between Paddington, Reading and Oxford. These replaced the ageing 'County' class '2221' tanks, which had formed the mainstay of these services for a number of years. The last working member of the class, No 2246, was withdrawn from Reading in December 1935, at which date Reading had no fewer than nine of the new '6100' class 2-6-2Ts in its allocation. By 1936 the 0-4-2T numbers had risen by the arrival of Nos 4807, 4809, 4847 and 4862. During 1938, Reading-allocated Moguls, together with their crews, started to work through to Redhill, and knowledge of the route by the Great Western crews was to be used to good effect during the war years.

By the start of World War 2, the allocation stood at 80, and included 'Star' No 4052 *Princess Beatrice* and 'Castle' No 4085 *Berkeley Castle*. The 'Star' was allocated away to Oxford in October 1940, and

Above:
Some of the SE&CR locomotive staff pose at Reading in 1915, with Wainwright 'C' class 0-6-0 No 684. Some of those identified in the group are Messrs P. Milsom, H. Hewett, B. Alder, R. Hockley, W. Woodham, W. Cotton, F. Bonney and R. Ward. *Courtesy Jack Hewett*

Right:
A pair of unidentified 'River' class 2-6-4T are seen here at Reading South in about 1927. These engines were used at Reading to work the heavy Birkenhead-Dover 'Continental' through service. *B. Davis collection*

during the same month six of Reading's 'Dean Goods' class were sold to the War Department, and subsequently saw service abroad. The loss of these was offset by the addition of a number of wartime loan locomotives, which included two LMS '2F' 0-6-0s Nos 3196 and 3616, and seven WD 2-8-0s. In 1944 five brand-new Swindon-built LMS-designed 8Fs Nos 8446, 8449, 8450, 8476 and 8479 arrived at Reading, and continued in use here until May 1947. Nationalisation saw the allocation standing at 99 locomotives — the highest ever total, which included 23 Moguls and 22 0-6-0PTs.

The early 1950s saw the withdrawal from Reading of some classes that had a long association with the shed. In December 1951 the last two 'Bulldogs', Nos 3453 *Seagull* and 3454 *Skylark*, were withdrawn, and in September of the following year the two ex-M&SWJ 2-4-0s Nos 1335 and 1336 left for the last time. Reading's 60-year association with the 'Dean Goods' class ended in February 1953 when No 2573 was withdrawn. The remaining decade passed without incident, although in 1957 as a sign of things to come four 350hp diesel shunters were allocated here for the first time. In October 1958 the Henley-on-Thames branch was dieselised. Reading had supplied engines for the branch from its opening in 1857. In June 1960 the 0-4-2T tradition at Reading finished, when No 1407 was withdrawn, having been a Reading locomotive since 1947. The end of the Great Western diesel railcars came during 1962 with Reading's last three examples being withdrawn in August, and one month later the last Mogul here, No 6391, was condemned. All was not gloom for during 1963 five 'Castles' were still active at Reading on secondary services and freights, having been displaced from the main line by the new diesel-hydraulics. However, 1964 was a bad year for

steam at Reading, with its gradual rundown prior to the closure of the shed on 2 January 1965. The few remaining 'Manors' were transferred away in May, and in June the last 'Castle' here, No 5039 *Rhuddlan Castle*, was withdrawn. By the end of the year the allocation, which in earlier days had reached almost 100, was now down to just 15, comprising 10 'Halls' and five '6100' class 2-6-2Ts.

Southern

The Reading-Redhill line had throughout its existence been classified as a secondary route of no great importance, and over the years the motive power has tended to reflect this, with the line becoming a veritable museum piece of both rolling stock and locomotives. Even today the Gatwick services are worked by 30-year old, life-expired DMUs.

Possibly the very first engines to be used at Reading were a pair of Bury singles, Nos 68 and 69, hired by the contractor during 1847 for the building of the Farnborough-Reading extension. Both were subsequently rebuilt as 2-4-0s, and No 68 is reported to have continued to work from Reading until its withdrawal in 1875. Records show a rather motley collection of locomotives working from Reading during these early years. It appears that the South Eastern pressed all manner of classes on to these early services, with various examples of Wilson 'Jenny Lind' and Stephenson-built 2-2-2s, together with Naysmith & Gaskell and Kitson-built 0-6-0s in evidence. By the 1860s some of the 'Forrester Goods' or 'Luggage' engines were on the line; these 2-4-0s had been constructed in 1845. By 1854 four examples of the Naysmith & Gaskell 'Hastings' class were at Reading for goods work. A pair of 'Folkestone' class 2-4-0s also appeared on Redhill services during January 1875. For many years Reading had an allocation of up to 10 Ashford-built '118' class 2-4-0s. These fine locomotives were used on a variety of duties and lasted for many years. In fact the very last 2-4-0 at Reading was No 245 of the same class. This was used for many years on banking and piloting duties, and was withdrawn on 4 March 1904. During 1897 seven Stirling 7ft 'F' class 4-4-0s were allocated to the line for Redhill services, with Reading having three, Nos 53, 88 and 228. Other notable examples working from Reading at this time were a number of Cudworth 0-6-0s. The Ash-Aldershot services were worked by examples of Cudworth-designed '205' and '235' class 0-4-2WTs. These were replaced during 1910 by Wainwright 'P' class 0-6-0Ts Nos 178 and 754. LSWR services to and from Waterloo at this time were generally worked by Adams 4-4-2Ts and 'Jubilee' 0-4-2s, together with

Drummond 'M7' class 0-4-4Ts, but by the end of World War 1 some of these had been replaced by the SECR 'F1' 4-4-0s. However, it was the 'M7s' that were to be the mainstay of the Waterloo services right up until the electrification of the line in 1939. For many years two LSWR locomotives from Nine Elms were outstabled at Reading for use on the Waterloo services.

Around the turn of the century, goods services over the South Eastern section were in the hands of Stirling 'O' class 0-6-0s of which 11 examples were based at Reading. During World War 1, a number of LSWR 'K10' 4-4-0s were based at Reading for working the heavy ammunition trains from the Midlands to Portsmouth Docks. By the 1920s goods services between Reading and Feltham were being worked by the then-new Urie 4-6-2Ts together with the 'S15' 4-6-0s. It appears that these engines were eminently suitable for the task as they were to form the mainstay of this service for almost the next 40 years. In 1926 four of the ill-fated 'River' class tanks, Nos A797, A805, A806 and A807, were allocated to Reading especially for the Birkenhead-Folkestone (the 'Continental') service. Upon withdrawal for rebuilding during 1928 they were replaced for a time by examples of ex-LSWR Adams 'Jubilee' 0-4-2 and Drummond 'K10' 4-4-0 classes. Incidentally many of the 'River' class 2-6-4Ts were stored at Reading prior to being taken to the works for rebuilding. During 1932 a pair of Stirling 'R1s' Nos 1708 and 1709 arrived at Reading especially for working the

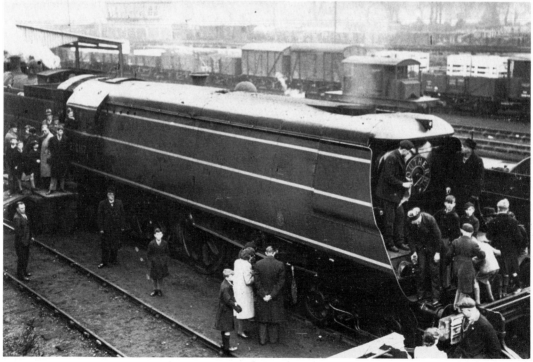

local service to Blackwater. In 1933 the allocation at Reading numbered 22, of which nine were 'F1' 4-4-0s, which still dominated the Redhill services.

Certainly the biggest change occurred in 1939 when passenger services to Waterloo were electrified, with a new half-hourly service throughout the day. Steam working over this route was now confined to the regular goods and parcel trains, which were usually in the hands of 'H15' and 'S15' 4-6-0s. The Redhill route, however, maintained steam haulage. During October 1945 Bulleid Light Pacific No 21C110 *Sidmouth* was involved in trials between Reading and Redhill, working four services daily. After World War 2 the 'F1s' still reigned supreme but in 1949 they were replaced at Reading by a number of 'B1' 4-4-0s. The last 'F1' at Reading, No 1231 was withdrawn on 12 March 1949 having travelled a total of 1,506,944 miles. By the early 1950s the 'B1s' had also departed, when the last one, No 31443, was withdrawn from Reading in February 1951. These were replaced by a number of 'D' class 4-4-0s, although by this time services were almost exclusively in the hands of 'U' and 'N' class 2-6-0s. Other classes, such as 'Q', 'Q1' and 'T9' appeared quite regularly on both passenger and goods services.

Above left:
The mainstay of South Eastern services from Reading for many years were the Stirling 'F1' class 4-4-0s. The fine lines of these locomotives can be seen in this picture of No 1195 at Reading in 1939. *C. R. L. Coles*

Left:
Bulleid Light Pacific 21C117 *Ilfracombe*, as yet unnamed, is seen here on a fund-raising visit to Reading South in aid of the St John ambulance service, March 1947. *Courtesy Jack Hewett*

Below:
The graceful lines of 'D' class 4-4-0 No 31574 are seen to good effect as it stands in the yard at Reading South on 20 April 1956. *R. C. Riley*

From 9 December 1953 the turntable at Reading was out of action due to repairs, and for several days all 11 daily services between Reading and Redhill were worked by 'M7' tanks. Ten locomotives were needed to cover the duties, so Nos 30109, 30110 and 30675 were sent to Guildford, Nos 30123, 30245 and 30377 to Redhill and Nos 30022, 30104, 30374 and 30667, to Reading. The partial closure of the shed in 1954 saw much of the allocation transferred away, the remaining 'D' class Nos 31496, 31586 and 31746 going to Guildford, 31737 to Tonbridge and 31075 and 31488 into store. The various 'U' and 'N' classes were distributed between Redhill and Guildford.

By the 1960s many of the older classes had gone and the 'U' and 'N' classes were supplemented with examples of Standard Class 4 2-6-0 and Class 5 4-6-0s, together with Standard 2-6-4Ts. In April 1961 six 'Schools' class 4-4-0s were allocated to Redhill and Guildford specifically for Reading line services. The three at Redhill generally covered the 7.27am up and the 5.25pm down services between Reading and London Bridge. It was, however, the old dependables, the 'U' and 'N' classes, that saw steam out on the Reading line. During the final week of steam passenger working prior to dieselisation, the following members of the 'U' and 'N' classes were noted at Reading, on Guildford and Redhill services: 'U' class Nos 31627, 31790, 31791, 31799, 31800, 31809 and 'N' class Nos 31405, 31408, 31816, 31831, 31858 and 31862. The dieselisation of the passenger services did not signal the end of steam at Reading South as for the rest of the year, goods services and diesel failures continued to bring steam into Reading over the old South Eastern route. As late as 21 August 1965, 'U' No 31639 worked the 17.08 passenger service to Redhill. In November 1966, nearly a year after the Southern shed had been demolished, Standard Class 4 No 76031 worked the Blisworth parcels between Reading General and Redhill. As a postscript, three ex-Reading locomotives have survived the cutter's torch: 'U' class No 31618 is now on the Bluebell Railway and

No 31806 on the Mid-Hants, whilst 'D' class No 31737, which was withdrawn in November 1956, is now in the National Railway Museum, York.

Although the South Eastern lines provided the bulk of the 'Southern' motive power at Reading, we must not forget that many LSWR engines ran into the Great Western station from Basingstoke. The Basingstoke branch was built and operated from the start by the Great Western, but in October 1932 the separate Great Western station was closed, and services from Reading were diverted into the LSWR station. From the turn of the century services from Portsmouth and Southampton to Reading were in the hands of Adams 'X2' and 'X6' 4-4-0 and 'A12' 0-4-2 'Jubilee' classes. These were eventually replaced by Drummond 4-4-0s of 'T9', 'K10', 'L11' and 'L12' classes. By the 1940s and early 1950s, local services to Basingstoke saw examples of the 'King Arthur' and 'Remembrance' classes as well as the usual 'N' and 'U' 2-6-0s. By the late 1950s, these had been displaced by examples of the Standard Class 4 and 5 4-6-0s, although the occasional 'King Arthur' still made an appearance. In 1962 steam was finally displaced from the services with the introduction of new Hampshire diesel units Nos 1127-1133, which were specially constructed at Eastleigh for 'Berkshire' line services. These are still operating the services today.

During the early years of this century, cross-country services via Basingstoke and Oxford were generally in the hands of Adams and Drummond 4-4-0s, but during the 1930s these were gradually replaced by the 'King Arthur' 4-6-0s. After World War 2 the 'Arthurs' were joined by examples of the 'Lord Nelson' class. These types continued to operate through to Oxford until the early 1960s; by this time, however, the service was generally in the hands of the Bulleid 'Battle of Britain' and 'West Country' Pacifics. In 1964 as weight restrictions over the route were eased, the Light Pacifics were joined by the heavier 'Merchant Navy' class. These types continued to operate the cross-country services, through Reading until steam traction was withdrawn from these trains from the start of the winter 1966 timetable.

The Diesel Era

It could be said that the diesel era at Reading started in October 1956, with the allocation of a pair of 350hp shunters Nos 13268 and 13269. By 1962 the diesel shunter allocation at Reading had risen to 15, with most of the yards locally being shunted by these types. Southern allocated examples and Drewry 204hp 0-6-0DMs had made the occasional appearance at Reading South yard from about 1955.

Left:
Guildford-allocated 'Schools' class No 30903
***Charterhouse* stands in the yard at Reading South,**
October 1961. *C. J. Blay*

Above:
An unusual visitor to Reading South is Standard '9F'
No 92217. Taken in November 1963, some wag seems to
have christened her the *(F)Lying Scotsman*. *C. J. Blay*

The author can well remember seeing Nos 13041 and 13042 of Feltham working in the South yard around this time.

Local Western Region passenger services in the Reading area were gradually taken over by Pressed Steel DMUs from the summer of 1960, and some 30 years later these same units are still the mainstay of the Thames Valley local services. By the end of Western Region steam traction in 1965, intermediate passenger services were in the hands of Beyer Peacock 'Hymek' Type 3s and Brush Type 4s. In 1968 a number of Class 31s were allocated to the Western Region, and these were used on both freights and intermediate passenger services. BRCW Type 3 locomotives had started to appear on inter-regional parcels and freight services through Reading from about 1962.

Western Region main line services were almost exclusively in the hands of 'Warship' B-B diesel-hydraulics, which were first introduced on to the services during 1958. In 1961 they were joined by the Class 52 'Western' and 35 'Hymek' diesel-hydraulics. During the late 1960s and early 1970s the up and down 'Cornish Riviera Express', which did not stop at Reading, was rostered for a pair of 'Warships'. The hydraulic era came to an end during the 1970s, with the withdrawal of the 'Warships' from the South-west route during 1972. The 'Hymeks', which had proved to be useful and reliable locomotives, lasted until 1975. The 'Westerns' survived a little longer, the last examples being withdrawn in 1977.

The withdrawal of the hydraulics was partially compensated for by the arrival during 1974 of the Class 50s, displaced from the newly-electrified West Coast services. HSTs were introduced on to the Bristol and South Wales services during 1976, their use being extended to Exeter, Plymouth and Penzance during 1979. Local Thames Valley goods services during the 1960s saw a succession of types including North British Type 2s, but these were gradually replaced during the early 1970s by the ubiquitous Class 31s. Certainly during the 1960s and 1970s it was possible to see a wide variety of BR diesel power at Reading. Today Reading has a locomotive allocation of just four Class 08s, to cover duties at Reading, Didcot and Oxford. The variety of motive power at Reading has diminished somewhat, with the constant procession of HSTs, Class 47s and Class 50s on passenger services, occasionally broken by examples of Classes 31, 33, 37, 56 and 59 passing through on the various freight services.

Industrial Railways

No book on the railways of Reading would be complete without mention of the several industrial systems that operated in the area. These ranged from just a couple of sidings to extensive track layouts. I have restricted my choice to these which actually operated their own locomotives. The largest of the industrial lines at Reading was operated by the biscuit manufacturers Huntley & Palmers.

Huntley & Palmers

Joseph Huntley started making biscuits and confectionery in his small shop at 72 London Street, Reading in 1822, and within a few years he was joined by his son Thomas who eventually took over

the running of the shop. Thomas concentrated on the baking and wholesale side of the business, starting by supplying his biscuits and cakes to the local residents and also to the travellers on the London-Bath stage coaches. His success was borne out by the fact that by 1839 he was supplying some

Below:
The consignment warehouse at Kings Road circa 1890, with cartons of biscuits being loaded, possibly for export. Prior to the arrival of the fireless locomotives, horses were used for wagon shunting.
T. Harden collection

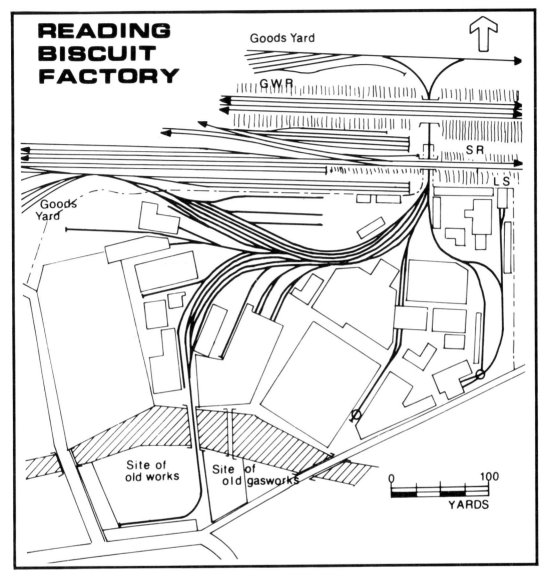

READING BISCUIT FACTORY

Goods Yard

GWR

SR

LS

Goods Yard

Site of old works

Site of old gasworks

0   100
YARDS

Above:
Map of Huntley & Palmers Reading biscuit factory.
Courtesy Industrial Railway Society

20 different types of his 'Superior Reading Biscuits' to over 100 retailers in the south of England. In 1841 he was joined in partnership by fellow Quaker George Palmer. Palmer was a trained confectioner who also had a great interest in mechanical things. The new partnership brought further success and by 1845 they were employing 16 staff. Palmer became the stronger influence in the partnership and decided the time had come to mechanise biscuit production. In 1846, flushed by their subsequent success, they purchased the former Bayliss silk crepe factory at Kings Road, close to both the Great Western and South Eastern Railways. They were to use the railways extensively to transport their products for well over 100 years. Biscuit production at the new factory was started in November 1846 and such was the popularity of their products that by 1856 they were employing 350 people. Thomas Huntley, who had not been in good health for a number of years, unfortunately died during the following year. George Palmer took over the running of the company together with his two brothers, but retained the original name in remembrance of his good friend and partner. The Huntley connection was still maintained as the company packed its biscuits in tins made by Huntley, Boorne & Stevens, a company founded by Thomas's brother Joseph.

Thomas Huntley's death did not apparently affect the running of the company as by 1860 Huntley & Palmers had become the largest biscuit manufacturers in the country, the workforce had risen to some 500, and they were producing over 100 different varieties of biscuit with sales amounting to some 3,210 tons per annum. By 1880 this annual figure had risen to 16,562 tons. The factory continued to flourish, moving much of its output by rail, and to effect this the company constructed within is 24 acre site its own private sidings. In

order to work these, in 1875 the company had purchased a pair of Black Hawthorn & Co of Gateshead 20ton 0-4-0ST locomotives, works Nos 352 and 375, becoming Huntley & Palmer A and B respectively. These were supplemented in 1900 by a pair of Peckett & Sons of Bristol 25ton 0-4-0ST Works Nos 831 and 832, which became C and D of the fleet. In order to accommodate these loco-motives, a small two-road locomotive shed was constructed at the north-east corner of the site and adjacent to the SE Wokingham line. During 1932 the company also purchased a pair of William Bagnall 0-4-0F locomotives, Nos 2473 and 2474. These were almost certainly to replace the pair of ageing Black Hawthorns, were numbered 1 and 2 by the company. The new locomotives were charged at various points around the site with high pressure steam. This took about 15 minutes, and gave them an average operating time of about 2 hours. The big advantage of these locomotives was, of course, their ability to operate within the various despatch warehouses without either fire risk or fumes. The two Pecketts were subsequently sold for scrap, No 831 in March 1939 and No 832 some 10 years later. It is known that the old south works was initially operated using some form of narrow gauge system but this appears to have been removed sometime before World War 1.

Left:

Locomotive A of the Huntley & Palmers fleet was a 0-4-0ST, built by Black, Hawthorn & Co, works No 1875. It is seen here at Reading around the turn of the century. *Museum of English Rural Life*

Below left:

The goods yard at Huntley & Palmers, again pictured around the turn of the century. Locomotive B is in the centre of the picture. *Museum of English Rural Life*

Below:

This view shows the tunnel connection between the Huntley & Palmers sidings and the low-level Great Western yard at Reading. The fireless locomotive, which only just seems to fit under the bridge is H&P No 2. *B. Davis collection*

During World War 1 the company did its part for the war effort, with part of the factory being given over to the manufacture of shells, machined parts for aero engines and rifle sights. Once the war was over, biscuit manufacture was once again expanded. Such was the expansion in production that by the 1930s in order to accommodate the incoming and outgoing goods the sidings had increased to some 7½ miles in length, with traffic to and from the complex running at some 15,000 wagons per annum. There is no doubt that much of the growth of Reading both in the late 19th century and also the early part of this century can be directly attributed to Huntley & Palmers, for at the height of their success they had over 6,000 employees, a figure that represented one quarter of the working population of Reading. As one journalist of the time put it 'Reading is the hub of the industrial south, and Huntley & Palmers ginger nuts hold it together'. George Palmer was a great benefactor to the town of Reading. In 1876 he presented to the town 14 acres of land at Kings Meadow and in 1889 a further 49 acres that became known as Palmer Park. Being a strict Quaker he insisted that no intoxicating liquor should either be sold or consumed within the parks. George Palmer died in 1897 and his son Ernest, who was also a director of the company, took over the mantle of his father as a notable figure in public life. He became a Baronet in 1916, and in 1933 he was elevated to the peerage taking the title Lord Palmer of Reading. His interest in the use of railways was reflected in the fact that he was a director of the Great Western Railway from August 1898 until his retirement in December 1943. The highest production figure at Reading was reached in 1917 with some 25,432 tons of biscuits being produced. In 1921

Below:
Biscuits for everyone! Tins of Huntley & Palmers 'Breakfast' biscuits being despatched from Kings Road. *B. Davis collection*

the company amalgamated with Peek Freans to form the Associated Biscuit Manufacturers and in 1960 W. & R. Jacobs also joined the fold, thus forming Associated Biscuits Ltd. During 1955 the company opened a new factory at Huyton near Liverpool, and gradually production was switched to the new plant. During March 1965 the rail connection to the nearby Western Region yard was closed, while the connection to the Southern yard lasted until February 1970. The two fireless locomotives were withdrawn during the same month; No 2 was scrapped but luckily No 1 was preserved and is currently on the West Somerset Railway.

After many years of being run down, biscuit production at Reading was finally discontinued during 1977. In 1982 the company became part of the American Nabisco foods group but during 1989 Nabisco sold the Huntley & Palmers Division to the French food giant BSN. Although the biscuit factory at Reading has now gone, the main office block in the Kings Road is still in use.

The Reading Gas Co

To the south-east of the Great Western main line and adjacent to the Huntley & Palmers system was the gas works of the Reading Gas Co. The original small plant was opened by the Reading Gas Light Co near the Bridge Street wharf in 1818. Gas lighting was first introduced on to the streets of Reading on 5 November 1819. This company was not the hive of efficiency and with its high prices a rival company, the Reading Union Gas Co, started production at its own small works at Gas Lane during 1830. This

arrangement resulted in cheap prices for the customers and low profits for the two companies. This situation could not last and eventually both companies amalgamated in 1862 to form the Reading Gas Co. In order to supply the expanding demand a new works was constructed under the Reading Gas Act of 1870, a short distance away from the old Union plant at Gas Lane. The new works were complete and ready for production by about 1872. The old gas works site was then absorbed into the nearby Huntley & Palmers complex. In order to supply the new works with coal, both high and low-level connections were made from the nearby SER Reading-Wokingham line, and a series of sidings, eventually almost ½ mile in length were constructed within the plant itself. Coal for the gas works was supplied twice a day with trip workings from the nearby SE yard, and the South Eastern locomotive would then be used to shunt the gas works sidings. For many years this working was in the hands of Stirling locomotives of the 'R' and 'R1' classes. These were replaced by examples of the LSWR 'G6' class. This class continued to be used on the gas works services until the 1950s, with 'G6' No 30270 together with ex-LBSCR 'E3' class 0-6-2T No 32170 being specifically kept at Reading for this duty. When these were not available a Great Western Pannier would occasionally be 'borrowed'. During 1947 the gas company purchased a Hibberd & Co 'Planet' 4-wheel diesel-mechanical locomotive No 3194 specifically for use on the low-level sidings.

Under the Nationalisation Act of 1948 the Reading Gas Co lost its individual status and became part of the newly-formed Southern Gas Board. In 1952 a second diesel locomotive, John Fowler 0-4-0DM No 4210072 was purchased, but it is not clear whether this was to replace or to supplement No 3194. It also appears that the Fowler was out of action for a time in 1966, as sister locomotive No 4210136 was at Reading on loan from Blackwater gas works for a couple of months.

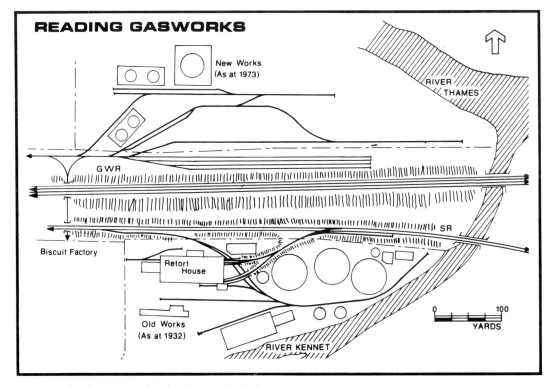

READING GASWORKS

New Works
(As at 1973)

RIVER
THAMES

GWR

SR

Biscuit Factory

Retort
House

0 ____ 100
YARDS

Old Works
(As at 1932)

RIVER KENNET

Gas production at Reading finally ceased during 1966 and the holders were used to store natural gas which was now being piped from Southampton. During the same year a steam naphtha reforming plant was opened opposite the old works, on the north side of the Western Region main line. This was served by new sidings that were connected to the Western Region low level yard at Kings Meadow. When gas production finished, the Fowler was switched to the new works, and it continued to give service here until rail traffic ceased in 1976, when it was withdrawn on 8 May. The old gas sidings had been taken out of use on 22 September 1970 and were finally removed during May 1975. Today the northern site is being developed as a business park but the old gas works of 1872 is still in use, albeit for storage only.

Earley Power Station

Another small industrial railway in the vicinity of Reading was situated within the Central Electricity Generating Board's coal-fired power station at Earley. This station has an interesting history, for it was originally scheduled to be built in South Africa. In fact two of the generators were actually shipped from this country, but were lost when the ship carrying them was sunk. The South African project was then abandoned and the remaining three generators were assembled to form a new power station at Earley, situated to the east of Reading,

Above:
Map of Reading gas works.
Courtesy Industrial Railway Society

Above right:
Map of CEGB Earley power station.
Courtesy Industrial Railway Society

Right:
Motor Rail Ltd 4-wheel diesel-mechanical No 3966. Built in 1939, this small locomotive was transferred to Earley in 1960, and was used intermittently until 1970. It was No 3 in the Earley fleet and is seen here on 24 October 1964. *P. J. Kelley*

and on the north side of the Great Western main line. Work on the station was started in 1942 with the final generator being commissioned in 1946. It became one of a series of small power stations built at this time, that also served as standby stations in the event of bomb damage to Battersea. In order to supplement the coal fired generators a new gas turbine-powered generator was constructed, and commissioned during 1964.

Earley was served by four exchange sidings, constructed by the GWR in June 1941. They were controlled from the nearby Sonning box, which itself was enlarged at the same time. From the outset the internal lines within the power station were worked by a Robert Stephenson & Hawthorn 0-4-0ST (Works

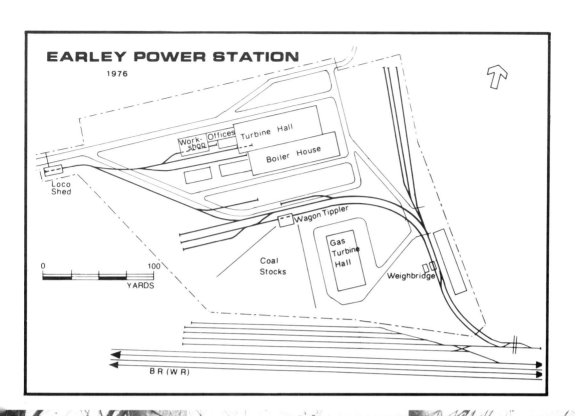

EARLEY POWER STATION

1976

Work-shop | Offices | Turbine Hall

Boiler House

Loco Shed

Wagon Tippler

Coal Stocks

Gas Turbine Hall

Weighbridge

0   100
YARDS

B R (W R)

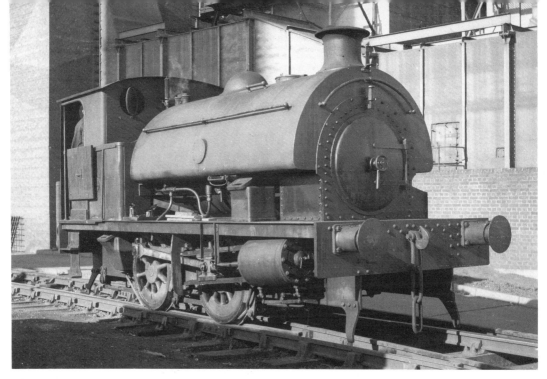

Above:
Earley power station 0-4-0ST No 2 pictured on 24 October 1964, was built by Robert Stephenson & Hawthorn in 1946. It operated at Earley from new until its withdrawal in April 1969. *P. J. Kelley*

No 7058), and this was joined in 1946 by a second RSH 0-4-0ST (Works No 7306). Both were purchased new and were numbered 1 and 2 respectively. To accommodate these two locomotives a small single-road locomotive shed was constructed to the west of the site. During the 1960s the two steam locomotives were joined on site by a pair of diesel mechanical shunters. The first, which arrived in 1960, was Motor Rail Ltd 0-4-0DM No 3966. Built in 1939, it was numbered 3 in the power station fleet. In 1968 it was joined for a short time by an Andrew Barclay 0-6-0DM No 422 which was numbered 4 in the fleet. The Motor Rail lay out of use for a short while before being transferred to the East Yelland power station in Devon in January 1970. During 1969, No 2, the newer of the two RSH saddle tanks was withdrawn from service. It was probably in quite a bad state mechanically as it was broken up on site during March of the same year.

Because of its small size, Earley power station had become uneconomical to run and following the construction of a new power station at Didcot, Earley became surplus to requirements and was closed in March 1976. The two remaining engines here were then sold, with RSH No 1 (7058), going to the Gwili Railway, and diesel mechanical No 422

(No 4) to Fathingstone Silos Ltd. The power station then lay derelict for a number of years before being partially demolished during 1983, and the whole site was finally cleared during July 1986. Today little trace of it exists and it is envisaged that the land may now be used for a science park.

CWS Coley

To conclude this chapter on the industrial lines, mention must be made of the Co-operative Wholesale Society Preserve works at Coley. The 'jam' factory, as it was known locally, was constructed in 1916 but because of the wartime shortage of both glass and sugar the opening was deferred until 1919. The factory during this time was used for aircraft construction. By 1920 production of jam was in full swing and the workforce of several hundred were producing some 1,728,000 jars of jam per year. In order to facilitate both the delivery of fruit and the despatch of preserves, the factory had its own private sidings. These left the Coley branch just to the south of the central goods depot. In 1939 the company purchased Hibberd & Co 4-wheel petrol mechanical shunter No 2213 for internal shunting. By the 1960s much of the incoming and outgoing goods had been switched to road transport, and in September 1964 the remaining sidings were closed. During the same month No 2213 was withdrawn and cut up on site. In 1967 the CWS made the decision to centralise its preserve production at the newly modernised works at Reddish (Manchester), and during the following year the works at Coley were closed.

Reading Today

Travellers arriving or passing through Reading today may be unaware of the rationalisation and closures that have taken place locally during the last decade. Gone are Suttons Seeds; the company moved to Torquay in July 1976, and the old trial grounds alongside the track are now an industrial estate. Much of the Huntley & Palmers biscuit factory has suffered the same fate since rail traffic ceased here in 1969. The manufacture of biscuits at the Reading plant finished in 1977. Today Huntley & Palmers are part of the giant French BSN group who currently still retain the administrative section in the old office block building at Kings Road. It has recently been announced that the new company have decided to move the administrative section away from Reading and that the Kings Road offices are to close.

The old Great Western signal works finally closed its doors for the last time during 1982 and on its site today stands a large postal sorting centre. Today many of the goods yards in the area are also closed. As mentioned in a previous chapter, the first two, at Scours Lane and West Junction closed in 1968. During the last decade, both of the lower yards together with the central goods depot have also

gone, and many of the sites are now covered with light industrial and commercial development.

The Southern station is now but a memory, its site covered by the modernistic Apex Plaza building. Part of the old yard is still in use however, with a pair of low-level electric unit stabling sidings alongside the 1899 incline junction. With all of these closures one would imagine a vast reduction in traffic locally, but surprisingly this is not the case, and it is probably true to say that today Reading has become the busiest station on the whole of the Western Region. The combination of the Southern services to Gatwick, Waterloo and Basingstoke, together with the ever increasing through freight traffic has made Reading a very busy and congested place indeed at times. Currently there are some 1,000 passenger, parcel train and light engine movements which pass through or use the station each weekday, and about 100 of these are freight trains. The failure of the

Below:
The interior of the Brunel Arcade contains many retail outlets as well as ticket and information points. *Author*

Western Region to rebuild the station in the 1960s put a terrible strain on the existing facilities, particularly in the area of the ticket office and station entrance hall. In 1982 plans were put forward to rebuild and modernise the old station, and preliminary work was started almost immediately. After many years of chaos for the traveller, the work was finally completed during 1989, culminating with the Queen opening the new Brunel Arcade on 4 April. The whole project involved the British Rail Property Board, InterCity Sector and Prudential Insurance. The whole complex was designed by British Rail architect Malcolm Wood.

The main station entrance complex measures approx 180ft × 100ft, and within its structure are situated 10 retail outlets, together with a below-

Above:
A pair of Railair link coaches stand outside the Brunel Arcade in August 1989. The ½hr interval service is operated by the Bee Line using five coaches and one spare. *Author*

Below:
The new ticket offices in the Brunel Arcade. *Author*

concourse Railcar lounge for passengers using the Heathrow Rail-Air Coach link. This service was inaugurated in 1967 and was initially operated by the Thames Valley Traction Co whose operations were taken over by the Alder Valley Bus Co in 1972, but since January 1987 the service has been operated by 'The Bee Line' which is part of the Berks & Bucks Bus Co. Coaches on this service run every half hour between 05.45 and 21.45 and currently carry over 300,000 passengers annually. At the station end of the arcade is a manned information point and, rather more importantly, no fewer than nine individual ticket outlets. Also situated alongside these are four of the latest mechanised customer-operated quick ticket machines. The arcade gives direct access to the nearby Apex Plaza office complex. This was also a part of the building programme and contains some 200,000sq ft of office accommodation. Other work completed at the same time included a complete refurbishment of the down main platform and bays. At the London end a new footbridge connects the Brunel Arcade with a new 1,400-car capacity multi-storey car park. An added feature is the use of escalators to gain access to the main platforms. The whole exercise cost some £20 million and should see Reading well into the next century. The old entrance building, which is Grade 2 listed, has been tastefully refurbished, and will probably see further use as additional office accommodation. Much of the administrative work at Reading is carried out in the large Western Tower building. Opened on 20 March 1967, it contains 15 floors and was, prior to its move to 125 House at Swindon in February 1984, the headquarters of the Western Region's London Division.

Although the signal works have long gone there is still a strong signalling presence at Reading with the Western Region S&T headquarters, design centre and signal training school all nowadays situated in the Tower building. However, during the last few years various other departments have moved away from Reading to Swindon, leaving several floors in the tower available for non-railway use.

Also situated at Reading is the area freight centre, which controls not just the immediate Reading area but the yards at Didcot and Oxford as well. Currently there are 900 staff employed in the Reading operating area, which since 1986 has expanded to include Oxford. This seems a far cry from the turn of the century when the GWR employed 2,000 men at Reading alone. The diesel depot currently provides employment for 66 members of staff, of which 21 are fitters, whilst the rest comprise supervisory, electrical and general maintenance staff. These undertake all manner of work from engine changes to complete repaints. Locomotive maintenance is not generally undertaken at Reading these days, but locomotives are still refuelled here using the new refuelling bay that was completed during 1987. The old refuelling shop has now been upgraded and is today used for the maintenance of engineering and PW vehicles. The diesel multiple-unit fleet currently numbers 47 sets,

Below:
The 1981-built extension at the diesel depot is now used for the maintenance of engineering vehicles. On 7 November 1989 the building was occupied by a PW crane and various track machines. *Author*

comprising 13 Metro-Cammell Class 101 and eight Gloucester Class 119 sets. These are used mainly on the Gatwick services, as the 21 sets are needed to cover the 15 working diagrams over this route. The remainder of the allocation comprises 26 Pressed Steel-built Class 117s for the Thames Valley local services, which now include the new service to Islip and Bicester. The five Class 08 shunters cover duties at Reading, Didcot and Oxford. Currently there are 125 drivers at Reading for Western Region services. Although the Southern shed has long gone, there are still 30 drivers based at Reading for the electric services to Waterloo, and these are now under the control of the area manager at Feltham. Situated within the diesel depot complex is the Western Region permanent way school. It was opened in 1985 and replaced the old PW school which was situated adjacent to the west cattle dock. The school has a staff of four instructors who undertake both initial training for all new recruits, and an ongoing training programme for all of the Western Region's 600+ PW staff. The adjacent yard is now given over to engineering use and is under the control of the area Civil Engineer. Shunting duties within the yard are, at the time of writing, undertaken by a Ruston & Hornsby PWM shunter No 97654. Another of these locomotives, No 97650, has been stored out of use for a number of years at the eastern end of the yard. Materials are conveyed between here and the engineer's depot at Gloucester via the 20.27

departmental service from West Junction to Gloucester New Yard.

For such a busy station Reading is currently run with a staff of just 38. This figure includes two station supervisors and there are also 10 employees on the commercial side and six per shift in the parcels office. This is a far cry from the days just before World War 2, when nearly 300 were employed at the station alone. Due to different accounting methods passenger numbers today are difficult to obtain, but an approximate figure of 40,000 passenger movements at Reading station each day would probably not be far out. This produces an annual revenue at Reading of about £16 million.

The arrival of the InterCity 125 High Speed Trains has improved services somewhat, with Reading being reached by the fast trains from Paddington in only 23min. Currently the fastest up service takes just 26min. The IC125s now form the bulk of the main InterCity passenger services to and from Reading with 52 up weekday trains to Paddington. Down services provide 16 trains a day to the West

Below:
The interior of the DMU servicing shed at Reading on 7 November 1989 with three Class 117 units under repair. *Author*

Country, giving an almost hourly interval service to Exeter. There are also 19 services daily to South Wales, 18 to Bristol and two each to Cheltenham and Hereford. There is an hourly Network Express service to and from Oxford and a two hourly service to and from Newbury. These have been in the hands of Class 50 motive power for a number of years but due to the increasing unreliability of these locomotives they are now being replaced by the ubiquitous Class 47s. On the electrified route to Waterloo journey times are somewhat longer, taking on average 74min, but it must be remembered that this service stops at most stations en route. The Thames Valley local services are still almost exclusively in the hands of the ageing Class 117 DMUs, which provide what is an approximately half hour interval service to both Paddington and Didcot. Henley is also well served with an hourly service from Reading throughout the day. On the Southern lines, electric services to and from Reading have changed little since their inauguration in 1939, with departures for Waterloo every half hour on weekdays, and hourly on Sundays. Guildford can be reached on the dieselised Gatwick services, of which there are currently 19 daily in either direction.

Reading West station is now only served by the Newbury and Basingstoke local services, a far cry from the days when cross-country trains avoiding the General station via the West Loop called here. Local services over the Basingstoke branch are still almost exclusively in the hands of the ageing Hampshire diesel sets, however the service has seen some improvement in recent years and currently provides what amounts to an hourly service each weekday. Local Berks & Hants line services to Newbury are currently operated using Pressed Steel Class 117 units. This service is extended to Bedwyn at peak times.

Today the cross-country services reverse at Reading with current practice being to run round the train (it used to be the custom to change locomotives here). These through services are now being worked almost exclusively by the long-range fuel tank-fitted Class 47/8s. During the next few years it seems many of these services may be operated by HST sets displaced from the newly-electrified Leeds and Edinburgh services. Certainly cross-country services to and from Reading have expanded over the years, and today there are daily through services to Liverpool, Manchester, Wolverhampton, Newcastle, York, Glasgow and Edinburgh and southwards to Poole, Portsmouth, Brighton, Folkestone and Dover.

Below:
The 10.22am HST service from Bristol Temple Meads to Paddington arrives at platform 5 at Reading on 29 August 1989. Station pilot is Class 47 No 47665.
Author

Of these the 09.18 Brighton-Glasgow, which commenced on 10 May 1988, and the 10.40 Poole-Glasgow have been named the 'Sussex' and 'Wessex Scots' respectively. Prior to the commencement of the Summer 1990 timetable these trains were split at Carstairs to provide a portion for Edinburgh, but this has now been discontinued and both services run through to Glasgow only. By way of compensation the Newcastle services have been extended to run through to Edinburgh. A feature of the current timetable is the 20.40 sleeping car service from Poole to Glasgow (06.20) and Edinburgh (08.25), this service is still split at Carstairs. Departure times from Poole have now been standardised at 40min past the hour and provide what is essentially an hourly service of cross-country trains.

As mentioned in a previous chapter, since April 1965 trains at Reading have been controlled from the Reading panel box, which has become the busiest on the Western Region. Open continuously, it is operated by four signalmen per shift aided by one relief signalman and a supervisor. The box now controls an area that stretches as far as Lavington on the Berks & Hants, to Milton, west of Didcot, and northwards to Appleford. Eastwards its control extends to Ruscombe and also from Southcote Junction to Basingstoke. It would appear that Reading power box may itself be due for

Above:
Class 47/4 No 47627 *City of Oxford* arrives at Reading on Tuesday 8 August 1989 with the 12.40 Poole-Liverpool Lime Street. *Author*

Above right:
The busy interior of Reading panel box in May 1989. On the right is the main panel controlling the section between Rushcombe and Didcot. In the left background is the separate panel for the Berks & Hants section. *Author*

Right:
Reading station viewed from the Caversham Road fire station. An HST awaits departure for the Southwest as a Class 56 arrives with some stone empties. *Author*

replacement in the not too distant future. During the week two station announcers are also employed here, one to cover Reading itself. The second announcer covers stations on the Berks & Hants line as far as Bedwyn, and Thames Valley line stations between Reading and Didcot. Situated under the power box is the area electricians' workshop.

Reading today has become an important interchange point for Royal Mail letter services. The large postal sorting building on the site of the old signal works has a floor area of 70,000sq ft. Reading is a concentration point for mail from Bucks, Berks,

Oxon and Wilts and each evening between 22.20 and 01.55 no fewer than six TPOs call at the station both to receive and to deposit mail. The first of these to arrive is the 19.15 Dover Priory-Manchester at 22.20. The two TPOs from Paddington, the 22.56 to Swansea and the 23.13 to Plymouth arrive at 23.26 and 23.44 respectively. Postal movements come to a head when all three of the up services, the 21.10 Manchester Piccadilly-Dover, 22.13 Plymouth-Paddington and the 21.49 Swansea-Paddington

arrive at Reading around 01.30, and accommodate three of the platforms simultaneously for about 20min. Another postal, formed partially of stock from the Swansea train leaves Reading for Bournemouth at 01.55. Certainly from the passengers' point of view it is a good job that the TPOs arrive during the night, for Reading never has had a separate platform solely for mail usage.

Most of the freight operation in the Reading area is now centred on Theale reception sidings, some 5½ miles to the southwest of Reading on the Berks & Hants line. This site started life as a waste tip and then from 1959 until 1972 it was used as a permanent way preassembly depot. Since then the site has been developed into a series of private sidings. Trains arrive here daily with oil for Murco Petroleum Ltd from Ripple Lane and Robeston, aggregates for both the Amey Group and Foster Yeoman from Westbury and Croft respectively and finally cement products for Blue Circle from Northfleet in Kent. Each of these companies has its own individual sidings at Theale. For such a busy yard it is surprising that a pilot locomotive is not based here. The growth in freight services locally should see the capacity of Theale yard increased in the not too distant future. The West yard at Reading is nowadays mainly used by the engineering section. Until recently a daily transfer freight between the military depots at Bramley and Bicester called here, but the closure of Bramley depot in 1987 has seen this working discontinued. However, some freights, including the Railfreight 'Satlink' service, still currently use the yard. The two lower yards at

Reading were finally cleared during 1987/88, and although a few sidings still exist at the eastern end of Kings Meadow, these are currently out of use. The rest of the yard is now almost completely covered by commercial development. Today freight traffic from the Southern via the New Junction, has almost dried up, with the only regular traffic being the daily cement train from Northfleet to Theale. This is not the case with the Basingstoke branch, which today is as busy as ever, with oil trains to and from Micheldever and daily freightliner services between Southampton and Lawley Street, Trafford Park, Coatbridge, Willesden and Stratford. The first three of these avoid Reading station by way of Oxford Road and West Junctions. Stone traffic from the Berks & Hants line to both London and the South

Midlands have been a regular feature at Reading for a number of years now. The construction of the new M40 motorway has seen additional services introduced between Whatley Quarry and railheads at Kidlington (Oxford) and Banbury.

What of the future? Reading is an expanding town, and to tap the new housing developments to the southeast of Reading a new station was opened at Winnersh Triangle on 11 May 1987. Berkshire County Council has discussed the possibility of constructing a new rapid transit rail system locally, similar in style to the Docklands Light Railway. But as yet this idea is still in the embryonic stage. It also seems that with the growth in traffic it will not be long before the general layout of Reading station itself will once again have to be altered. One idea currently being looked at, which would increase the capacity of the station, is to demolish the buildings running along the Caversham side of platform 9, to allow a new platform face to be opened up, which would then become platform 11. Should this occur it may then be possible for the Post Office to install some kind of direct conveyor from the nearby sorting office to this platform, supplementing the existing subway link. Another proposal currently under discussion is the possible electrification of the section between Wokingham and Guildford. Once agreed, the work could be completed during 1991. The completion of both of these proposals could see the electrified Gatwick services running via the old skew tunnel into a newly electrified platform 11. The extra length of this platform could also mean that at peak times it could be used by some of the Waterloo services, which due to heavy loading now need strengthening up to 12 coaches.

Yet another proposal is for the electrification of the Basingstoke branch. Should this happen, one can but speculate about the possible need to form some sort of electrified connection through the station between this and the Wokingham line. At the time of writing it has been announced that the Thames Valley services are to be modernised using the new turbo-diesel Class 165 trains. These it seem will take over all of the local services during the next few years. Second-generation Class 166 turbos are due to replace the locomotive-hauled Network Express services between Paddington, Oxford and Newbury during 1993.

Below:
Class 47/4 No 47549 *Royal Mail* **stands at platform 9 at Reading with the 13.43 Bristol Temple Meads-Paddington parcels on Tuesday 24 October 1989.**
Author

Locomotive Allocations

The following locomotives were noted working at Reading during March 1840:

'Fire Fly' class
Fire Fly
Tiger

'Star' class
Dog Star
Evening Star
Morning Star

Unclassified
Ajax
Atlas
Mars
Planet

Reading GWR Broad Gauge Allocation 27 July 1850

2-2-2 'Fire Fly' class
Fire King

2-2-2 'Priam' class
Medea

0-6-0 'Pyracmon' class
Mammoth

2-2-2T 'Sun' class
Aurora
Comet
Eclipse
Meteor
Sun

2-4-0T 'Leo' class
Etna
Sagittarius

Reading GWR Broad Gauge Allocation 19 July 1862

2-2-2 'Fire Fly' class
Lucifer
Phoenix
Vulture

2-2-2 'Priam' class
Dart
Firebrand
Lynx
Panther
Pluto

0-6-0 'Premier' class
Ajax
Bergion

2-2-2T 'Wolf' class
Eagle
Vulcan

Reading GWR Allocation 1 January 1901

0-6-0 Armstrong 'Standard Goods'
25
52
117
503
680
786
1100
1202

0-6-0 'Dean Goods'
2346
2435
2493
2504
2518
2522
2532
2534
2562
2567

0-6-0 '927' class
933

2-4-0 'River' class
76 *Wye*

2-2-2 '157' 'Cobham'
163

0-6-0 '360' class
362

2-4-0T 'Metro Tank'
458
629

0-4-2T '517' class
1471

0-6-0ST '1016' class
1023

0-6-0ST '1076' class
1080
1166
1263
1270
1578
1636
1657

0-6-0ST '1661' class
1672

0-6-0ST '1813' class
1826

0-6-0ST '1854' class
1719
1890
2-4-0 '3201' class 'Stella'
3201
3502
3503
3509
4-2-2 'Achilles' class
3025 *St George*
4-4-0T '3521' class
3526
0-4-0ST Ex-South Devon Railway
1328
Total: 44

Locomotives outstabled:
BASINGSTOKE
2-2-2 '378' class 'Sir Daniel'
380
0-6-0 'Standard Goods'
504
2-4-0 '3232' class
3242
HENLEY-ON-THAMES
0-4-2T '517' class
1482

Reading GWR Allocation 1 January 1920
0-6-0 'Standard Goods'
693
795
882
1207
2-4-0 '481' class 2-4-0
487
0-4-2T '517' class
548
2-4-0T '455' class 'Metro'
1459
3593
0-6-0PT '1016' class
1026
0-6-0PT '1076' class
740
1172
1242
0-6-0PT '1854' class
1725
1770
1896
0-6-0PT '2021' class
2112
2-4-0 '2201' class
2206
2213
2214

4-4-2T 'County' Tank
2235
2236
2241
0-6-0 '2361' class
2369
0-6-0 'Dean Goods'
2337
2431
2451
2463
2471
2479
2512
2561
2572
0-6-0ST '2721' class
2757
2-8-0 '2800' class
2802
2836
2-8-0 'ROD' class
3027
3028
3029
3031
2-4-0 '3232' class
3232
3233
3234
3236
3249
4-4-0 '3252' class
3268 *Chough*
3281 *Cotswold*
3283 *Comet*
4-4-0 'Bulldog' class
3356 *Sir Stafford*
3374 *Walter Long*
3384 *Swindon*
3386 *Paddington*
3407 *Madras*
3421
3426
3437
2-4-2T '3600' class
3611
4-4-0 'City' class
3715 *City of Hereford*
4-4-0 'County' class
3821 *County of Bedford*
4-4-0 'Atbara' class
4128 *Maine*
4129 *Kekewitch*
4130 *Omdurman*
2-6-0 '4300' class
4316
4383

Locomotives outstationed:
BASINGSTOKE
4-4-2T 'County Tank'
2233
HENLEY-ON-THAMES
2-4-0T '455' class 'Metro'
625
1455
LAMBOURN VALLEY
0-6-0T '850' class
1953

Reading GWR Allocation January 1930

2-4-0T 'Metro' class
615
1415
3599
0-4-2T '517' class
568
1430
0-6-0T '655' class
1743
0-6-0T '1016' class
1066
0-6-0T '1076' class
956
1240
1248
1295
2-4-0 '1334' class
1336
0-6-0T '1813' class
1832
0-6-0T '1854' class
1797
1877
4-4-2T '2221' class
2229
2233
2237
2239
0-6-0 'Dean Goods' class
2305
2343
2447
2471
2479
2512
2572
0-6-0 '2361' class
2369
2376
2-6-0 'Aberdare' class
2609
0-6-0T '2721' class
2757
2784

4-6-0 'Saint' class
2926 *Saint Nicholas*
2981 *Ivanhoe*
2-8-0 'ROD' class
3025
3026
2-6-2T '3150' class
3166
4-4-0 'Duke' class
3285 *Katerfelto*
3286 *Meteor*
3290 *Severn*
4-4-0 'Bulldog' class
3302 *Sir Lancelot*
3319 *Weymouth*
3323 *Etona*
3325 *Kenilworth*
3326 *Laira*
3350 *Newlyn*
3364 *Frank Bibby*
3382
3390
3394 *Albany*
3404 *Barbados*
3411 *Stanley Baldwin*
3427
3434 *Joseph Shaw*
3448 *Kingfisher*
3450 *Peacock*
2-4-2T '3600' class
3600
3610
4-4-0 'City' class
3712 *City of Bristol*
4-4-0 'County' class
3813 *County of Carmarthen*
3820 *County of Worcester*
3825 *County of Denbigh*
3830 *County of Oxford*
2-6-0 '4300' class
4359
4364
4375
6312
6315
6345
6356
6380
8305
8308
8313
8338
8383
2-6-2T '5101' class
5147

Locomotives outstationed:
BASINGSTOKE
0-6-0 'Dean Goods' class
2404

4-6-0 'Hall' class
4966 *Shakenhurst Hall*
LAMBOURN
0-6-0T '850' class
1921
HENLEY-ON-THAMES
2-4-0T 'Metro' class
616
WALLINGFORD
0-4-2T '517' class
1469

Reading GWR Allocation January 1940

2-4-0 '1334' class
1335
1336
0-6-0T '2021' class
2055
0-6-0 '2251' class
2208
2252
2264
2299
0-6-0 'Dean Goods'
2559
2-8-0 'ROD' class
3025
3026
3047
4-4-0 'Bulldog' class
3386
3418 *Sir Arthur York*
3419
3426
4-6-0 'Star' class
4052 *Princess Beatrice*
4-6-0 'Castle' class
4085 *Berkeley Castle*
2-6-0 '4300' class
5356
5375
5380
5385
6312
6313
6320
6359
6383
6393
7318
9309
9313
9315
9317
9318
9319

0-4-2T '4800' class
4809
4844
4847
4848
4-6-0 'Hall' class
4931 *Hanbury Hall*
4989 *Cherwell Hall*
4992 *Crosby Hall*
4994 *Downton Hall*
4995 *Easton Hall*
5901 *Hazel Hall*
5933 *Kingsway Hall*
5948 *Siddington Hall*
5959 *Mawley Hall*
5973 *Rolleston Hall*
5986 *Arbury Hall*
0-6-0PT '5700' class
3715
3727
3783
5761
5762
5763
5766
5772
7708
7777
7788
9722
9791
2-6-2T '6100' class
6100
6109
6117
6131
6136
6140
6153
6154
6159
6162
6163
6165

Locomotives outstationed:
BASINGSTOKE
2-6-0 '4300' class
6363
9305
4-6-0 'Hall' class
4914 *Cranmore Hall*
0-6-0PT '5700' class
3770
2-6-2T '6100' class
6130
HENLEY-ON-THAMES
0-4-2T 4800 class
4837

Reading (WR) Allocation January 1950

2-4-0 '1334' class
1335
1336

0-4-2T '4800' class
1444
1447

0-6-0 '2251' class
2208
2245
2264
2299

0-6-0 'Dean Goods' class
2573

2-8-0 'ROD' class
3025
3047

4-4-0 'Bulldog' class
3454 *Skylark*

0-6-0T '5700' class
3697
3715
3723
3736
4609
4661
4665
4670
5762
5763
5766
5772
7708
7777
7788
9722
9749
9763
9791

2-8-0 '2800' class
3840
3841
3845
3846

4-6-0 'Castle' class
4085 *Berkeley Castle*
5036 *Lyonshall Castle*

4-6-0 'Hall' class
4920 *Dumbleton Hall*
4931 *Hanbury Hall*
4939 *Littleton Hall*
4943 *Marrington Hall*
4962 *Ragley Hall*
4989 *Cherwell Hall*
4994 *Downton Hall*
4995 *Easton Hall*
5901 *Hazel Hall*
5933 *Kingsway Hall*

5948 *Siddington Hall*
5956 *Horsley Hall*
5957 *Hutton Hall*
5959 *Mawley Hall*
5973 *Rolleston Hall*
5979 *Cruckton Hall*

4-6-0 'Modified Hall' class
6968 *Woodcock Hall*
6996 *Blackwell Hall*
7919 *Runter Hall*

2-6-0 '4300' class
5375
6312
6334
6363
6366
6379
6383
6393
7318
7320
9303
9307
9313
9318
9319

2-6-2T '6100' class
6100
6101
6105
6130
6145
6153
6162
6163

4-6-0 'Grange' class
6802 *Bampton Grange*
6864 *Dymock Grange*
6865 *Hopton Grange*

0-6-0 '9400' class
9410
9411
9412
9420

Ex-GWR Diesel Railcars
W1
W19
W22
W37
W38

Reading (WR) Allocation October 1964

2-6-2T '6100' class
6103
6107
6134
6135
6161

4-6-0 'Hall' class
5971 *Merevale Hall*
6924 *Grantley Hall*
6938 *Corndean Hall*
6953 *Leighton Hall*
4-6-0 'Modified Hall' class
6963 *Throwley Hall*
6974 *Bryngwyn Hall*
6991 *Acton Burnell Hall*
7904 *Fountains Hall*
7910 *Hown Hall*
7919 *Runter Hall*
0-6-0DE 350hp shunter
D3030
D3268
D3269
D3518
D3831
D3948
D3953

Reading South Allocation
January 1898

2-4-0 '118' class
30
34
63
75
86
113
132
186
219
242
245
4-4-0 'F' class
53
88
228
0-4-2T 'Q' class
40
141
200
0-6-0 'R' class
125
152
0-6-0 '59' class
59
70
150
Total: 21

Below:
Stirling 'R1' 0-6-0 No 1070 stands at Reading South on 5 August 1939. Behind can just be seen 'F1' No 1231.
V. R. Webster

Reading South Allocation January 1933

0-6-0 'C' class
1225
0-6-0T 'R1' class
1047
1174
1708
1709
0-4-2T 'R' class
1658
1659
1662
1666
1667
1672
4-4-0 'F1' class
1025
1042
1056
1074
1117
1118
1143
1187
1190
2-6-0 'N' class
1861
Total: 21

Reading South Allocation January 1946

0-6-0T 'G6' class
258
260
4-4-0 'F1' class
1042
1043
1060
1062
1078
1079
1140
1156
1183
1188
1195
2-6-0 'U' class
1610
1611
1620
1627
1628

2-6-0 'N' class
1857
1860
1861
Total: 21

Reading South Allocation May 1949

0-6-0T 'G6' class
30258
4-4-0 'B1' class
31217
31443
31446
31448
31451
31452
31455
2-6-0 'U' class
31610
31611
31614
31615
31797
2-6-0 'N' class
31857
31860
31861
31868
0-6-2T 'E4' class
32487
Total: 18

Reading (SR) Allocation November 1954

0-6-0T 'G6' class
30160
4-4-0 'D' class
31488
0-6-2T 'E3' class
32168
0-6-2T 'E4' class
32501
32502
Total: 5

Reading (SR) Allocation November 1955

0-6-0T 'G6' class
30160
0-6-0T 'E3' class
32168
Total: 2

Appendices

Opening Dates of Great Western Lines

Twyford-Reading	30 March 1840
Reading-Steventon	1 June 1840
Reading-Hungerford	21 December 1847
Southcote Junction-Basingstoke	1 November 1848
Reading West Junction-Oxford Road Junction	22 December 1856
Reading West Junction-Staines & Wokingham Railway (SER)	1 December 1858
Hungerford-Devizes (Berks & Hants Ext)	11 November 1862
Reading New Junction-South Eastern Rly	17 December 1899
Coley Branch from Southcote Junction	4 May 1908
Spur Junction GW line-Southern line	16 March 1941

Opening Dates of Southern Lines

Reading, Guildford & Reigate Railway

Reading-Farnborough	4 July 1849
Redhill-Dorking	4 July 1849
Farnborough-Ash Junction	20 August 1849
Dorking-Shalford Junction	20 August 1849
Reading-Redhill (throughout)	15 October 1849

London & South Western Railway

Ash Junction-Farnham	8 October 1849
Wokingham-Reading	9 July 1856

Signalboxes at Reading

Western Region

	Opened	Frame (levers) at closure	Closed
Scours Lane Junction	c1893†	52	26/4/65
Reading West Junction	c1893†	134	26/4/65
Southcote Junction	c1896†	35	26/4/65
Oxford Road Junction	1906†	25	26/4/65
Reading Main Line West	c1896†	222	26/4/65
Reading Goods Lines West	c1897	43	26/4/65
Reading Middle Box	1912†	21	6/6/59
Reading Main Line East	c1896†	115*	26/4/65
Kennet Bridge	c1899	8	13/2/61
Sonning Sidings	1893	54	13/2/61

*This box also had a 36-lever power frame added in 1941
†These were later replacements for earlier boxes.

Southern Region

	Opened	Frame (levers) at closure	Closed
Reading Station South	c1898	65	5/9/65
Reading Junction	17/12/1899	66	5/9/65
Reading Spur Junction	16/3/41	52	5/9/65

Early GWR boxes closed pre-1948

	Opened	Frame (levers) at closure	Closed
Reading High Level	c1890	25	c1925
Goods Lines East	c1898	57	c1923
Cow Lane	c1874	21?	c1910